Leading Beyond Excellence

Learn 7 Practical and Spiritual Steps to Spiral Yourself to the TOP

Executive Publishers International
3525 Del Mar Heights Rd. #205
San Diego, CA 92130

ISBN: 0-9726075-9-5

Distributed by PGW

Book cover design and layout: Jessup-Owen Design Studio

Printed in the USA

This book is dedicated to all who dare to lead beyond excellence and answer "Yes" to the call to rise to their highest potential.

Inspired by Mr. F. Sheridan Garrison
and the Leadership Team at FedEx Freight

TABLE OF CONTENTS

ABOUT THE AUTHOR

Dr. Lisa Williams MBA MA

Dr. Williams is a respected researcher, national columnist and award-winning speaker. She is the CEO of Williams Research, Incorporated, a premier leadership development firm. As a former professor at Penn State University and an endowed chair holder, she has dedicated her life to educating and developing excellence in future and current leaders. Major corporations and President Clinton's Commission on Critical Infrastructure Protection have sought her advice. Dr. Williams' research has practical and global implications and, as such, she has spoken to audiences in the United States, Belgium, Austria, Canada, the United Kingdom and Australia.

Dr. Williams has been given the highest honor bestowed upon a faculty member - an endowed chair. Actually, Dr. Williams has been given this honor not once, but twice, in three years. As the first female to hold a multimillion-dollar endowed chair in her field, the first

African-American female to graduate from The Ohio State University's Marketing and Logistics Department and the youngest in her discipline to become a full professor, she has committed herself to exceptional scholarship. In fact, her accomplishments were recognized when she was given the American Marketing Association PhD Project Trailblazer Award.

Peers and students alike recognize her as a leader in the field of business and supply chain management. She has received teaching awards and recognition from The Ohio State, Penn State and the University of Arkansas. Dr. Williams has been ranked by the most prestigious journal in the field for the number of articles published. Her research has been published in the *Journal of Marketing Channels, Journal of Business Logistics*, the *Transportation Journal, The International Journal of Physical Distribution* and *Logistics Management* and the *International Journal of Logistics Management*. Her column "Profiles in Leadership" is published in the *Supply Chain Management Review Magazine*. While featured in many magazines for her expertise in business, she is also known for her ability to motivate executives, future leaders and audiences of all sizes.

ACKNOWLEDGMENTS

I have to admit, writing the acknowledgements section is difficult. I am unsure I can find the words to truly express my gratitude to all who have assisted in this project.

To those who have been with me from the beginning, my family, thank you. To my mother, Mary Moore, you were the first to demonstrate that there was a powerful force guiding the world. Your love, guidance and nurturing have made all the difference in my life. Thank you from the depths of my heart. To my sister, Tamra, you have been there from the childhood traumas of "Dippity Do" to the adventures in adult life. Thank you for giving help every time I asked. To my son, Matthew, I thought I had experienced life before you entered my world. I was wrong. You have single-handedly taught me love, patience and compassion. Thank you for enriching my life. To my aunt, Joanne Ward, you were always a source of inspiration in difficult times. Your kind and humorous advice inspired me and I try to emulate you daily. To my aunt, Brenda Barnes, you have taught me generosity and kindness. You are my role model for successful businesswomen. To my uncle, Bill Wayne, thank you for helping to create within me the desire to strive for goals I had only dreamed of. A great deal of my personal drive I owe to you. Thank you all.

To those who are the wind beneath my wings, my friends, I do not believe any one person has been blessed with more loving supporters. To Angela Farrar, you are one of the wisest people I know; wisdom pours from you without effort. You are "coach to the world," and I am grateful to have you in my life. To my earth angel, Katherine Guendling, you have been my light in writing this book. Your constant smile and positive attitude encouraged me to continue when I thought there was no chance of completing the book. Alisa Hudson, thank you for constantly reminding me of the Power within me. You gave me the ability to see a higher Power was at work in my life. Your gentle eyes and supportive words helped inspire me to complete this book when I had reached exhaustion. Thank you for the collaboration and hours of conversation. To my girl, Sandra Hickman, thank you for being there and understanding the rocky part of my life's journey. I am glad you and I found smooth pavement. We can say, "Life is good!" To all my friends, I say, "thank you," for being the embodiment of wisdom.

To those I have met recently, Danny Williams, thank you for love and laughter which has opened me up to being the best I can be. To Almon Gunter, thank you for the motivation and the idea for this book. You have forever changed my life. To Tom Morris, PhD; Juanell Teague; and

Charlotte Shelton, PhD, who are successful writers and speakers committed to making the world a better place, thank you for showing me the way. To Bob Buford, thank you for personifying a significant leader and letting me know that living by higher ideals is possible for us all. To Mary Manin Morrissey and Michael Beckwith, thank you for sharing life-changing insights at the Possibilities Conference, which gave me the courage to reach for my highest goals. To Connee Chandler, Kenneth Clarke, Marshall Gabriel, Tammy Miller, Christian Sørenson and Cindy Stutting, thanks for your guidance. It means more than I could ever express. To Sharon LaFlore, thank you for holding the mirror up to me. To Derrick McKisick, thank you for being a wise sounding board, and to Patricia Benesh for your hours of tireless editing and encouragement. To Jerry and Ester Hicks and the guidance of Abraham, thanks for your joyful wisdom. To Carlos Santana, thank you for setting the example that life, love and purpose can be one beautiful expression. Lastly, to my colleagues, students, former professors, teachers and numerous executives, thank you for contributing to the wise lessons I have learned. To all of you I say, "Namaste."*

* "Namaste" means "The divine in me honors and blesses the divine in you."

FOREWORD

I have a quick question for you.

Are you willing to invest 10 minutes a day – that's right, just 10 minutes a day – for one year to change your life?

If so, you're going to love this book.

In 1995, I had the privilege of being inducted into the University of Illinois, Chicago, Entrepreneurial Hall of Fame. Since then I've spoken to lots of groups about the topic of success. Sometimes after these talks people come up to me or send me e-mails asking for advice on how they can develop their leadership skills, how they can be more effective in life or how they can achieve success in life. While I'm humbled that they would even ask, frankly I'm a bit discouraged. After all, time is limited and there is only so much advice one can give.

Having finished Lisa's book, I now know what I will do. When people ask questions about leadership, effective life strategies or success in life, I'll encourage them to pick up a copy of her book.

Here is why I'm so excited about this book. First, the book is like a roadmap. It gives you a structure or route for pursuing success. You start your week off with a great quote addressing a theme of utmost importance to living a successful life. You spend seven days reflecting on the insights that this quote elicits and develop an action plan for putting the thought into action. You make personal observations about how the insights and action steps have impacted your life. Then you move on to the next great quote or thought.

Second, it encourages you to develop the greatness that lies within you. I love to dream and think about what the future holds – especially in the context of a relationship with God, the Creator. In this book you'll read about this God in a manner that people of all faiths can grasp. Call Him what you will, the fact is, you were built for accomplishment and designed for success by the Creator who affirms, "you are precious and honored in His sight." (Isaiah 43:4)

Armed with this knowledge and with the roadmap in your hand, the rest is up to you. Remember, a roadmap isn't any good unless you use it. So put this roadmap to work for you today. I congratulate you on investing 10 minutes a day toward your success. Here's to future victories in the game of life.

Michael Regan
President, Tranzact
December 2002

AUTHOR'S NOTE

It is possible to achieve what some say is impossible and what others simply cannot see. You can spiral into a significant leader who makes life better for yourself and blazes new trails for others.

As a researcher and seeker of a more joyous and fulfilled life, I have searched for years to discover a way of having a successful career and a satisfying life. This book, *Leading Beyond Excellence,* is a unique combination of a cutting-edge leadership program and a self-discovery process.

You have known there is more for you, more to achieve, more to do and more to have, but until now you didn't have the tools. This book is written in a concise, clear and organized manner, so you can read, grasp and implement the information. You and I live in a fast-paced environment; events, situations and life are evolving at what seems to be warp speed. The "MTV Effect" has shortened our attention span. By dedicating only 10 minutes a day you can make noteworthy improvement in your leadership style and the joy you experience in life.

Unfortunately many colleges and universities do not offer leaders tools for development; in fact, most college curriculum focuses on training instead of education. While leadership training is a key to improving efficiency of routine tasks, it offers limited help in solving today's problems, which are usually supply chain-related issues, spanning across two or more companies within highly competitive markets. Such challenges require self-awareness, innovative thinking, courageous actions, strategic foresight and the ability to garner team support. In other words, they require exceptional leadership qualities – qualities that I believe everyone can develop but no one can be taught.

You will find the information in this book valuable regardless of your leadership position. The essence of leadership is the ability to influence others. Whether you are a senior executive, a new hire or an embedded leader, the seven-stage Spiral of Influence can assist you in unlocking your highest potential, enabling you to reach your goals.

This book can be used as a stand-alone resource for leadership development, a supplement to a university curriculum and a complement to a corporate training program. Readers often make an intimate connection with this book, allowing it to serve as a journal of their personal development. Through deliberate and disciplined adherence to the daily 10-minute exercises, you will learn how to spiral yourself to significance. As you complete the program outlined here you will see the boundaries between personal and professional life fade into one life, one purpose, and one experience – joyful success. You can realize your personal dreams. You can achieve your professional goals. You can live the life you desire. You can have a more successful career while leading the way for others to see greater possibilities for themselves. You can lead beyond excellence.

I wish you success.

Sincerely,

Dr. Lisa Williams, MBA, MA
San Diego, CA
November 8, 2003

INTRODUCTION

"Leading beyond excellence" is the process of moving from fear-based self-denial to love-based self-appreciation.

No one in history had run a four-minute mile. Many tried, but no one succeeded – as well it should be, according to experts. Doctors and physiologists thought the body and mind would surely rebel against the strains of such a feat. Commentators said it was inconceivable for an athlete to run that fast. Everyone began to think a four-minute mile was impossible to achieve. Even valiant attempts by John Landy, one of the world's greatest milers of the time, proved unsuccessful.

Previous failed attempts cemented the common belief that the four-minute mile could not be run. However, a young medical student at Oxford University, Roger Bannister, had a personal dream of breaking the barrier. He let go of the opinions of others and followed his dream. He focused his thoughts on breaking the barrier and intensified his physical training for the race.

On March 6, 1954, he stepped onto the track, ran a mile in 3:59:4 and made history. He did it! Bannister had broken the four-minute mile barrier. Despite common belief, there was no mental or physical breakdown. In fact, he probably never felt more alive. We can only imagine how he felt achieving his goal. We do know the impact his accomplishment had on others. Through his leadership, a goal that took more than 1,000 years to achieve was broken in just 46 days by another runner motivated by Bannister's achievement.

Bannister's unquenchable thirst to reach his personal dream allowed him to achieve his goal. His ability to rise to the call, to be more than he had been, enabled others to see the possibility of achieving their dreams. Today breaking the four-minute mile is commonplace.

Do you want to have more? Do you want to be more? Do you want to achieve more? Do you want to grow into your best? Do you really want to help others achieve more? Do you want to joyfully succeed in life? If you answered "yes" to any of these questions, welcome. You are in the company of great philosophers like Emerson, Whitman and Thoreau; eminent theorists like Einstein and James; distinguished inventors like Edison, Bell and the Wright Brothers; and celebrated businessmen like Walton, Dell and Bezoz. At some time in their lives they heard the call for more too, and they, like you, answered "yes."

They followed their passions to reap rewards from

life and had the courage to forge their unique path and create a common good for all. In college many thought Michael Dell was foolhardy to think he could build a computer in his dorm room that would compete with IBM, but he did! No one believed a poorly educated mechanic could design and build the automobile, but Henry Ford did it! When Pierre Omidyar decided to create an electronic auction everyone thought he was crazy. But within a few years he was worth four billion dollars and had created eBay. As they followed their dreams, they improved the lives of society. They motivated others. They are significant leaders. They are trailblazers.

Now it is your opportunity to heed the call to achieve your dreams, whether big or small. You can be a trailblazer. Trailblazers are leaders who see and create new paths in achieving professional goals and personal dreams by releasing fears and accepting their true self-expression. This book will introduce you to a program and a philosophy that will help you answer the call. Leading beyond excellence is within your reach. You can lead others to achieve by motivating them. The best way to do this is to be inspired. By making steps toward your dreams you can inspire yourself, energize others and move your organization forward faster and more efficiently than ever.

To be a trailblazer you must lead yourself through the process of self-discovery. "Leading beyond excellence" is the process of moving from fear-based self-denial to love-based self-appreciation. The result is a trailblazer. When leaders are unsure of their worth, they usually try to win and hold onto the opinions of others. As leaders develop into trailblazers, they become less reliant on others and more confident of their own thoughts.

This book is designed to be your personal prescription to leadership significance. Significant leaders feel fulfilled, passionate and joyful in their professional and personal lives. The boundaries between work and pleasure blur. They live in creative energy, always finding new ways to improve life for themselves and others. They exceed limitations and begin to realize they can achieve what others had deemed impossible. Dean Kamen, the modern-day Edison, dreamed of a way for the physically disabled to climb stairs. Some saw this idea as an oxymoron; Kamen saw it as a possibility. In 1999 he unveiled the 3000 IBOT – a personal transporter that climbs stairs. His roles as inventor and advocate are intertwined – his own passion for technology and its practical uses has driven his personal determination to spread the word about technology's virtues and by so doing to change the culture of the United States.[1]

Research for the Book

The information in this book is an accumulation of years of research and exclusive interviews[2] with many world-class leaders like: H. Lee Scott, CEO of Wal-Mart; Keith Harrison, Global Supply Officer of Procter & Gamble; Sheridan Garrison, Member of Federal Express Board of Directors; Nathan Harris, VP of Sales, TissueLink; Wayne Paul, VP of Home Depot, and William "Gus" Pagonis, a retired three-star U.S. Army General and now President of Sears Logistics and Senior VP, Supply Chain Management for Sears.

The concepts are based on insights from leaders and the latest discoveries in leadership development. To excel in your role as a leader, you must learn how to positively influence others. The first step in attaining this goal is to discover, understand and shed old thoughts and behaviors limiting your impact. An assessment tool has been developed to assist you. By taking the Spiral of Influence Survey you will gain valuable insights into your professional and personal life. After uncovering your hidden drives and personal challenges you will be guided on how to move yourself to a more

To be a leader is to discover, understand and shed old thoughts and behaviors limiting your impact

desirable location on the Spiral of Influence by following 10-minute exercises, many of which you can do from your desk.

Timeless wisdom from great leaders and thinkers will accompany your personal development. Their words will inspire and encourage you on your journey to connecting with the Power within you. This Power, paradoxically, is in you and yet it is bigger than you. The core of a trailblazer's success is the guidance and confidence created through this connection.

William Turner, CEO of Wisdom Television, was offered millions to sell his cable television station. The attorneys drew up the papers, the employees agreed and all seemed well, except to Turner. He went home feeling there was something about the deal that just didn't "sit right" with him. When he thought about selling the company he had a queasy feeling in his stomach. After much deliberation, he decided not to sell. He trusted his "gut instincts." Within weeks another buyer offered him three times the previous bid for his business.

Jeff Bezos, who in 1990 was the youngest Vice President at Bankers Trust, left the secure financial world, moved to Seattle Washington and started an online company because he trusted his internal Power. With a 70 percent probability of failure, it is no surprise his primary investors were his parents. Bezos was not discouraged; on the contrary, he was confident of his decision. His internal guidance was right; he achieved his dreams, his parents reaped their returns and the world benefits from the products and services of Amazon.com.

Relying on your Power will give you the assurance and direction to achieve your purpose in the face of insurmountable odds. In essence, leading beyond excellence is synonymous to rising to your highest potential by freeing yourself from the limitations set by others. Other people, who may simply want to protect you, ultimately prevent you from discovering yourself and what you can achieve. Significant leadership beckons you to be you. It urges you to release yourself from your self-imposed box and free yourself from the opinions of others.

Bill and Dave met on a camping trip after graduating with electrical engineering degrees. In 1938, during the Great Depression, with a budget of $500 they decided to start a new business in Dave's garage. Many thought they were insane, but Bill Hewlett and Dave Packard proved they were not limited, even by economic conditions.

When leading beyond excellence, you will discover that people follow you not because of your position or because you have set the rules. They follow you because of who you are and what you represent. They know you have made your own personal journey. They sense and feel it. They are attracted to it. They see your vision, and through commitment, not coercion, they strive for more because you have shown that more is possible.

Opportunities for Supply Chain Leaders to Lead Beyond Excellence

Over the decades I have had the honor of teaching undergraduates, masters and doctoral students, as well as executives. While each group of students has a special gift to contribute to the world, I am particularly awed by the opportunity presented to business leaders. The sheer number of people leaders influence within their organizations and throughout their supply chains today is unmatched in history. Through networks of organizations, supply chains have a common objective: to satisfy the global customer. In meeting this objective, today's leaders are influencing employees within their organization and those within their trading partners'. If they are given the tools, supply chain leaders have the opportunity to meet organizational objectives, influence positive worldwide change and provide unparalleled benefits to society.

H. Lee Scott, who spent 20 years of his career in transportation and logistics, is now the President of the world's largest retailer, Wal-Mart Stores. Keith Harrison, Global Supply Officer of Procter & Gamble; Wayne Paul VP of Home Depot; Sheridan Garrison, Member of Federal Express Board of Directors; and Gus Pagonis, a retired three-star U.S. Army General and now President of Sears Logistics, to name a few, are highly developed supply chain leaders that are making positive changes to supply chains and society.

Embedded Leaders

All leaders can achieve success regardless of their current level. Thus, the Spiral of Influence is appropriate for leaders at the executive level, those embedded within multiple layers of the organization and those newly hired. Within many organizations embedded leaders go unnoticed and undeveloped. They are among the most influential individuals because of the trusted relationships they develop at multiple levels throughout the organization. Through their powerful connections, they are the true communicators within an organization. They are well-trusted for their knowledge and information. Co-workers seek their advice because they usually know where the "minefields" are. They know the internal politics, other leaders' hot buttons and the way to effectively get things done within the organizational structure. They are immensely valuable in creating synergistic relationships and implementing organizational change.

Embedded leaders are among the most influential individuals.

Thus, it is necessary for leaders to be developed at all levels of the organization from the clerk to the CEO, because each has the unique ability to influence others. Some leaders have official designation; others do not. However, the commonality among leaders is that they influence and motivate others. They lead best when, like Roger Bannister, they achieve their goals.

Why Lead Beyond Excellence?

Under the premise that leaders are perhaps the single-most important factor in effecting organizational and societal change, I conducted this research from a desire to develop a model of exceptional leadership. This concept shows that by following their dreams, trailblazing leaders can be more, achieve more and get more while inspiring themselves and motivating others. It is the real meaning of Win-Win-Win-Win relationships. The trailblazer wins by achieving his or her dreams; the observer wins by becoming energized to achieve more; the organization wins by becoming more efficient and society wins through improved products and services.

> *Achieve more and get more while inspiring and motivating others.*

This is different from the popular view that defines leaders as people who must sacrifice their desires for the well-being of others. After talking with many world-class trailblazers, I believe their success is not based on losing themselves, but in finding themselves and living their passions. The Walton Family, while generous philanthropists, has been criticized for not giving more of their vast wealth. However, they believe they have already contributed the greatest gift: an example that achieving your dreams is possible.[3] Sam Walton was raised in America's heartland and lived through the Great Depression. Armed with a dream and borrowed money, he created Wal-Mart, the world's largest retail empire. He has shown the way. Not content with a modicum of retail success, Sam Walton went beyond success and beyond excellence to make himself and many Wal-Mart associates very happy and wealthy.

In his autobiography, *Made in America: My Story*[4] Walton said, "Somewhere out there right now there's someone – probably hundreds of thousands of someones – with good enough ideas to go all the way. [Wal-Mart] will be done again, over and over." It is my hope in writing this book that more leaders will abandon the notion that they must "fall on the sword." Instead they will embrace this principle: They have the greatest leadership impact when they are achieving their dreams.

Some leaders, who do not understand this principle, believe it is their dreams versus those of their co-workers. In the recent scandals of WorldCom and Enron, the leaders thought to realize their dreams of financial wealth and security, they had to take from their co-workers. Nothing could be farther from the truth. Had they understood the leadership acumen of Aaron Feuerstein, CEO of Malden Mills, the outcome for everyone would have been drastically different.

Malden Mills, like many American textile companies, was barraged with competition. Many other mills had closed or moved overseas. Aaron had dreamed of making his late father's business a success. After investing millions to develop revolutionary new products, the inconceivable happened; it all went up in smoke. On December 11, 1995, a fire ripped through the plant, burning most of it to the ground and putting 3,000 people out of work. As CEO Aaron Feuerstein and many of the co-workers watched the smoldering embers, it seemed like a sad finish to a long and hard struggle. Then he uttered, "This is not the end."[5] With those words, he became a restorer of hope, a legend among leaders and a hero among his employees.

What distinguishes Aaron Feuerstein and other trailblazers like him is that they see themselves and co-workers as part of a cohesive network of dream makers. Feuerstein could have taken the insurance money and settled into an easy retirement. Instead he used it to pay the workers while the plant was being rebuilt. After reopening Feuerstein said, "Before the fire, that plant produced 130,000 yards a week. A few weeks after the fire, it was up to 230,000 yards. Our people became very creative. They were willing to work 25 hours a day."[6]

Managers See Problems: Trailblazers See Possibilities

Managers are concerned with ensuring the goals of the organization are being meet. They have the position in the organization that gives them the authority to accomplish objectives through others. Managers enforce established rules and are almost solely focused on improving "the numbers."

Leaders set corporate culture and establish an environment where people can meet the corporate goals. Leaders are concerned about motivating others. They set corporate direction, and lay out plans for meeting or exceeding last year's goals. They usually create based upon past performance. Leaders build from the past while the trailblazer is creating from the possibilities.

Trailblazers set expectations based on the future, not the past; on opportunities, not limitations. Paraphrasing the words of Robert Kennedy at the 1968 presidential campaign, there are those who look at things the way they are, and ask why...while trailblazers dream of things that never were, and ask why not?

However, they are not renegades. They are people who are doing the personal work, releasing their fears, reviewing the facts, and moving forward in expressing their vision. They are willing to trust themselves in achieving their dreams and assist others in doing the same. Trailblazers are not superhuman; in fact, they make mistakes. Not only do they learn from their mistakes, but they share their lessons with others. When asked by a reporter if he was thinking about giving up after failing over 5,000 times to invent the incandescent light bulb, Thomas A. Edison responded, "Young man, I have not failed. I have simply found 5,000 ways that won't work. I am 5,000 ways closer to finding what will."

Trailblazers set expectations based on the future, not the past—on opportunities, not limitations.

Additional distinctions between managers, leaders and trailblazers are made in the table on the following page. The categories for manager and leader are from the classic book *On Becoming a Leader*, by Warren Bennis.[7]

Table 1 Differences between Managers, Leaders and Trailblazers

MANAGERS	LEADERS	TRAILBLAZERS
The manager administers.	The leader innovates.	The trailblazer inspires himself and motivates others.
The manager maintains.	The leader develops.	The trailblazer allows the genius within himself and others to grow.
The manager asks how and when.	The leader asks what and why.	The trailblazer, synthesizing intellect and intuition, asks what do you think and how do you feel.
The manager has his eye always on the bottom line.	The leader has his eye on the horizon.	The trailblazer has his eye on the vision of what is possible.
The manager accepts the status quo.	The leader challenges it.	The trailblazer is a consensus builder enabling everyone to see the possibilities.
The manager is the classic good soldier.	The leader is his own person.	The trailblazer is continually growing in self-knowledge and thus into a joyful person and successful leader.
The manager does things right.	The leader does the right thing.	The trailblazer sees the good in every situation and acts to maximize the greatest good.

COMMITMENT

The First Step to Leading Beyond Excellence

"Desire is the key to motivation, but it's determination and commitment to an unrelenting pursuit of your goal - a commitment to excellence - that will enable you to attain the success you seek." Mario Andretti, U.S. auto racer

You are choosing to embark on a path that will lead you to the success you desire. Commitment is the first step to leading beyond excellence. You are pledging success to yourself. No one is looking over your shoulder. No one is evaluating your progress. You are committing to yourself. You will set your goals. You will determine your progress. You will succeed if you are determined and committed to do so. To demonstrate your commitment to your success in this program, please read, date and sign the form on the following page.

As a further demonstration of your commitment, please go to **www.LeadershipCommitment.com** and sign up. It's free. To show our commitment to helping you achieve your goals you will receive:

1. A beautiful Leading Beyond Excellence Certificate suitable for framing. It is a wonderful reminder of the process you have begun.
2. Weekly messages to motivate and inspire you to continue toward your goals.
3. Access to exclusive interviews with exceptional leaders.

Leading Beyond Excellence Commitment:

I am ready to achieve leadership significance and my personal dreams. I fully commit to my personal success. Thus, I promise to:

1. Perform the 10-minute exercises daily.
2. Form a Leading beyond Excellence And Development (L.E.A.D.) Team for support and encouragement.*
3. Refrain from thinking or speaking unpleasant thoughts about myself and others.
4. Surround myself around goal-oriented, positive people.
5. Remind myself daily of how good I will feel when I have achieved my goals.
6. Not allow negative thoughts, actions or words of others to deter me from achieving my goals.
7. Stop trying to figure out how everything will come together, trust the process and look for evidence that my desires are coming.
8. Do something every day that makes me joyful and happy.

Signed this ______ day of ____________20______

____

Your signature

*More information about your L.E.A.D. Team can be found in Appendix B.

SPIRAL OF INFLUENCE

SPIRAL OF INFLUENCE

The Spiral of Influence is a personal tool for leaders to become trailblazers. Through a series of steps, leaders begin to develop their confidence and self assuredness. They begin to trust their instincts, change their limiting thoughts and move toward their dreams. As trailblazers set their visions and achieve their goals, they simultaneously pull everyone up to a higher standard – to a level where others begin to see themselves achieving what once seemed impossible. Everyone began to think a four-minute mile was impossible to achieve. Even valiant attempts by John Landy, one of the world's greatest milers of the time, proved unsuccessful, until Roger Bannister.

People follow leaders who have confidence in their abilities, calmness in spirit during times of unexpected events and who are inner-directed, but focused outward on the benefits of others.

The bottom line is that people follow leaders who have self-confidence in their abilities and goals, calmness of spirit during times of unexpected events, and who are inner-directed, but focused outward on the benefits of others.

Successful leadership is not about doing; it is about BE-ing. It is not just about imitating the actions of trailblazers. Instead it is essential to embrace and operate from the principles that produce their success. It is embodying the character, competence and self-knowledge inherent in excellent leadership. The purpose of the Spiral of Influence and the 10-minute exercises is to assist leaders in BE-coming exceptional leaders.

The process of leading beyond excellence is best represented by a spiral because it is a continual process of inner development and outer influence. The Spiral of Influence is a multidimensional figure representing the personal development of leaders and their impact on the organization and supply chain. Leaders will naturally move forward on the spiral unless they choose not to evolve and stop the learning process. As with any aspect of life, leaders have control over their progression. Remaining static and even descending the spiral is an option.

I can assure you, based upon the research and conversations with trailblazing leaders, the payoff in professional achievement and personal fulfillment more than pays for the effort of moving forward. If you are willing to progress on the Spiral of Influence, and invest in your personal development, you will, with the guidance provided in this book, improve your leadership skills, increase your Spheres of Attraction and enjoy a more gratifying professional and personal life.

The Spheres of Attraction

The spheres of attraction refer to an individual leader's ability to positively attract people and situations that support and encourage the organization's longevity, profitability, authenticity and channel relationships. It is based upon the science of attraction, sometimes referred to as the "law of attraction." In fact, this law is the basis of relationships, organizations and even our universe.

According to Wheatley and Kellner-Rogers:[8]

> There is an innate striving in all forms of matter to organize into relationships. There is a great seeking for connections, a desire to organize into more complex systems that include more relationships, more variety. This desire is evident everywhere in the cosmos at all levels of scale. Particles are attracted to other particles and so create atoms. Microbes combine with other microbes to create capacities for larger organisms. Stars, galaxies and solar systems emerge from gaseous clouds that swirl into coherence, creating new forms of energy and matter. Humans reach out to one another and create families' tribes and work organizations. Attraction is an organizing force of the universe...Attraction has created the universe we know. (p. 30)

According to the law of attraction, things attract

like things. Thus, each sphere of attraction represents the degree to which leaders can attract people and conditions to achieve organizational goals. The most powerful attracting force at the discretion of leaders is the mind and its thoughts. Leaders ascending the Spiral of Influence will experience positive changes in their thoughts, which, through the law of attraction, will draw similar people and increase their spheres of attraction and organizational impact.

Organizational Impact

Leaders following the Spiral of Influence can have greater impact on the organization's longevity, profitability, authenticity and relationships. Listed below are four cornerstones by which leaders following the Spiral can impact the organization. The cornerstones are depicted by the shaded quadrants within each sphere.

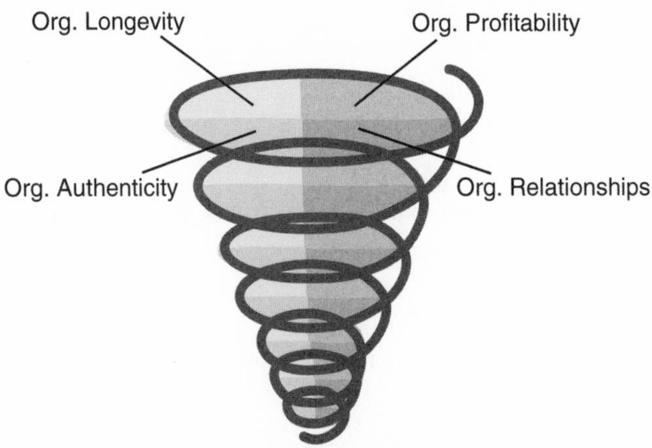

Organizational Longevity

Organizational longevity is the length of time the organization remains a profitable and vital entity. As leaders invest in personal development, they are able to positively impact others to increase creativity and productivity. This enables their companies to overcome competitive pressures and maintain customers through new products and services.

Organizational Profitability

Organizational profitability is the financial or monetary gains received from the marketplace in exchange for producing a valuable product or service. As leaders move along the spiral, they will be able to develop and effectively implement programs, which can reduce costs and increase revenues.

Organizational Authenticity

Organizational authenticity is the environment where people feel they can be genuine with their thoughts, ideas and feelings. They perceive they can freely voice their opinions without fear of being condemned or criticized.

Research has long suggested that this can create good working conditions and improve employees' job satisfaction.[9]

Organizational Relationships

Organizational relationships are interactions within the organization and between the organization and its supply chain partners. When leaders have invested in personal development, they are more likely to have the skills required to build collaborative relationships.

Significant Leaders Are Not Trained, They Are Developed – But Where?

Unfortunately, many colleges and universities do not offer leaders tools for development; in fact, most college curriculum focuses on training instead of education. Although the terms education and training are used interchangeably, they actually have distinct meanings. Training involves making a person proficient in a particular task or operation, while the word "education" comes from the Latin word *educare*, which means "to draw forth from within" the establishment of the principles and the regulation of the heart.[10] It involves self-trust and expression of ideas. While most corporate development programs are excellent at imparting information about internal operations and management skills, many do not focus on the actual development of leaders.

Now its your time to further develop your leadership. By taking the survey below and following the 10-minute exercise program outlined later, you will take a step toward developing yourself into a significant leader.

SPIRAL OF INFLUENCE Survey

PART ONE

To help determine your current stage on the Spiral, please respond to statements by circling a "1" if you strongly disagree with the statements, a "7" if you strongly agree with the statements or a number in between, depending on your agreement or disagreement.

Read each statement carefully.

Do not go back to answer questions.

	Strongly Disagree ◂ ▸ Strongly Agree
1. I believe everyone should be a lifelong learner.	1 2 3 4 5 6 7
2. I can't understand why rich people can be stressed and unhappy to the point of committing suicide.	1 2 3 4 5 6 7
3. I always buy the product insurance when I buy products. You can never have too much insurance.	1 2 3 4 5 6 7
4. Some people have a hard time thinking of anything appropriate to talk about when they first enter a new or strange group of people. I don't have that problem; I enjoy meeting and talking with strangers or a new group.	1 2 3 4 5 6 7
5. I think everyone should be heard – even those who have little or no experience on the subject.	1 2 3 4 5 6 7
6. I am impatient with people who ask too many questions.	1 2 3 4 5 6 7
7. I have a hard time saying "no" to people I know; thus, I often take on too much.	1 2 3 4 5 6 7
8. I stay one step ahead of my bills, so I find it challenging to save for the future.	1 2 3 4 5 6 7
9. I like "being in the know" at work because it's exciting to share information with my co-workers.	1 2 3 4 5 6 7
10. I like it when I have clearly laid-out plans to follow.	1 2 3 4 5 6 7
11. Whether I am at work or home, my principles always guide my actions.	1 2 3 4 5 6 7
12. If I didn't have money worries I would not be stressed.	1 2 3 4 5 6 7

	Strongly Disagree ◂ ▸ Strongly Agree
13. I think it is sad about the human rights violations in other countries; we should get involved and help.	1 2 3 4 5 6 7
14. I understand how to manage stress in my life.	1 2 3 4 5 6 7
15. I think people who give up everything – job, houses and security – to follow their dreams are to be admired.	1 2 3 4 5 6 7
16. It is hard for me to understand how old people who have worked all their lives end up on welfare.	1 2 3 4 5 6 7
17. Totally integrating my work and my passions has become easy for me.	1 2 3 4 5 6 7
18. Although we have many problems here in the U.S., I think we must always be concerned about poverty in other parts of the world.	1 2 3 4 5 6 7
19. If rules are not clear, life seems very chaotic.	1 2 3 4 5 6 7
20. I have a panic attack if I have to voice an opposing view to management.	1 2 3 4 5 6 7
21. The old adage, to save 10 percent for a rainy day, is great advice.	1 2 3 4 5 6 7
22. I avoid things that make people upset with me. It is important that I get along with everyone.	1 2 3 4 5 6 7
23. Traditions are very useful for me because they tell me what is expected of me and what I should do.	1 2 3 4 5 6 7
24. People who believe that money is made to be spent and enjoyed are irresponsible.	1 2 3 4 5 6 7

	Strongly Disagree ◂ ▸ Strongly Agree
25. The best contribution I can give to the world is to be at peace.	1 2 3 4 5 6 7
26. I become very fearful if I walk into a room where I don't know anyone.	1 2 3 4 5 6 7
27. I believe the media overreacts about environmental issues.	1 2 3 4 5 6 7
28. When I have a compelling drive to do something, I must do it or I feel stress.	1 2 3 4 5 6 7
29. I believe people who think their thoughts alone impact others are very wise and insightful.	1 2 3 4 5 6 7
30. My company has many goals, and I am integral to achieving them.	1 2 3 4 5 6 7
31. I need to know not only "what" to do, but "why" it is important.	1 2 3 4 5 6 7
32. The best thing about reaching a goal is knowing that I was important in achieving it.	1 2 3 4 5 6 7
33. I thoroughly enjoy having intellectually stimulating conversations.	1 2 3 4 5 6 7
34. It is extremely important to me that I am recognized for the work I do.	1 2 3 4 5 6 7
35. Because I do not believe teenagers should smoke, even if it makes good business sense for me to send cigarettes to other countries where teenagers may have access to cigarettes, I would not do it.	1 2 3 4 5 6 7

PART TWO

Please add your circled responses from the survey.

For example:
If you circled a 3, 5, 7, 2 and 4 for the questions 2, 8, 12, 16, and 24, then for stage one you would have a total of 21 (3+5+7+2+4 = 21).

Leadership Stage	Add your responses to questions	Total of responses
Stage 1: Survival	2, 8, 12, 16, 24	
Stage 2: Security	3, 21, 10, 23, 19	
Stage 3: Social	4, 7, 9, 22, 26	
Stage 4: Self Esteem	5, 20, 30, 32, 34	
Stage 5: Search	1, 6, 14, 31, 33	
Stage 6: Surrender	11, 15, 17, 28, 35	
Stage 7: Significance	13, 18, 25, 27, 29	

The highest sum indicates the stage which best represents you. Those who lead beyond excellence are driven to achieve their personal dreams and professional goals, which they begin to understand is really one goal – *freedom to live their lives.* If you desire, you can reach your preferred location on the spiral. By moving along the Spiral of Influence your thoughts will change. As you live your life, achieving your dreams and goals, people will notice and will be drawn to your Sphere of Attraction. Then you can be the teacher who educates not only in words, but in the life you live. Read the description for your stage and begin the process of leading beyond excellence.

SPIRAL OF INFLUENCE: Stages

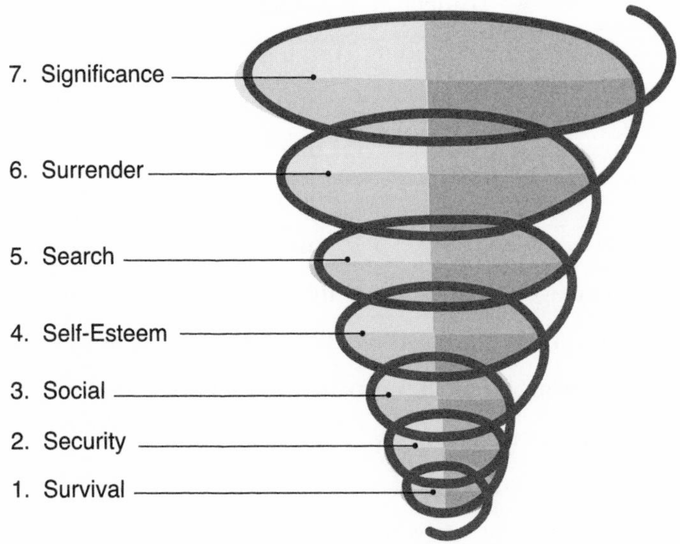

STAGE ONE: Survival

The first of the seven stages is survival. Leaders at this stage are simply trying to hold on to their position. They have little to no experience in leading others. Perhaps one was a great forklift operator and another was a customer service representative, so management promoted them to leadership positions. While they were great in their previous positions, with little to no leadership experience, they were are likely to feel "in over their heads." For example, one of my former graduate students, Mike Manin, was a great student. He was intelligent, personable and respected by his peers, teachers and university administration. It was no surprise he was hired in a leadership position by a Fortune 200 company after graduation. However, being a successful student had in no way prepared him to lead a staff of six people. Overwhelmed, he worked long hours at high stress levels, which resulted in ulcers and other stomach ailments. Although he asked to attend leadership seminars, his management thought he would "get the hang of it" with a little more time.

Typically stage one leaders act out of fear.

Feeling closed-in and thinking his co-workers would detect his inexperience and would undermine him, Manin took a new stance. He became hard, demanding and coercive with his staff. Instead of being cohesive, the department became competitive, resulting in an atmosphere of disrespect and distrust. When the numbers were less than expected, Manin turned up the pressure. He couldn't afford to lose the position; his workers simply had to work harder. Eventually, the work environment became unbearable, two of his top co-workers left the department and Manin's superiors began to lose faith in him. After only 18 months Manin left the company. If Manin had had the education and the tools to develop into a leader, the outcome could have been different.

Typically stage one leaders act out of fear. They close communications, decreasing trust and eroding collaboration within the organization. At this stage, leaders must focus on releasing fear and becoming open to sharing with co-workers and learning from successful leaders.

The survival stage can be a fertile learning ground. Take the case of H. Lee Scott, now CEO of Wal-Mart. Unlike Manin, Scott received the opportunity and support to develop as a leader. In an interview with Scott, he recounts a story in which lack of leadership experience caused him to clamp down on input from his co-workers.

"When I was 30, I thought I knew everything," he admits.

This attitude kept him from listening when truck drivers came to him with challenges or suggestions. The result: the drivers proceeded to Sam Walton's office under the open-door policy and asked that Scott be fired. Sam paid close attention to the drivers, then called Scott in to listen.

Scott remembers, "After the drivers finished, Sam asked me if I could change. I said, 'Yes, sir.' Then he had me stand there and shake their hands and thank them for using the open-door policy." Scott adds, "As you might expect, things improved greatly after that."

As an added benefit, Scott became close friends with many of those drivers. This experience and others helped him reach the brown-paneled office once occupied by Sam Walton. As head of the world's largest retailer, Scott leads Wal-Mart with the lessons he learned from his experiences at the survival stage.

Unsuccessful leaders at the survival stage often behave by closing the flow of meaningful communication. This creates a counterproductive environment. The leader's Sphere of Attraction is rather small. Co-workers will follow the survival leader because of the leader's ability to affect their performance reviews – not because the leader has a vision. If any vision is apparent it is consumed with helping the leader keep his position.

An example of a leader that successfully made it through stage one is King Hussein's son, Abdullah. Near the end of his reign, King Hussein surprisingly appointed his 37-year-old son as his successor. The expected successor, Hassan, the king's brother, had 35 years of experience in domestic and foreign policy. In comparison, Abdullah was known in Jordan as the President of the National Football Federation. He had little political experience, but his proponents said he would learn with the help of veteran politicians who had worked with his father. And so he has. The new king, with leadership tools, has become confident in his role and is developing into his new position successfully.

To move from stage one to stage two leaders must release their fear of failure. They must begin to see life as a learning opportunity and heed the advice of successful people whom they admire and respect.

A rule of thumb for taking the advice of others: Would I want to live their lives? Would I want to switch places with them? If the answer is yes, listen to their advice. As you progress on the spiral, you will soon have more confidence in following your own instincts and have less need to rely on the advice of others.

STAGE TWO: Security

At the second stage, security, leaders are not concerned as much with simply surviving. They have begun to understand some of the basic tenets of leadership. They are beginning to relax in their new roles. Now the preoccupation turns to security. They are fearful they will lose their lose budgets, people or other resources relative to others in the organization.

They feel they can't afford to trust their co-workers.

As such, these leaders sometimes display qualities of micromanaging. They feel they can't afford to trust their co-workers. This type of behavior leaves employees feeling devalued and frustrated.

In an interview, Wayne Paul, VP of Transportation of Home Depot, talked about the effects of a micromanager. Paul discovered firsthand the negative impact such a style can have on employee morale and creativity. "A micromanager can single-handedly reduce an employee's creativity and job satisfaction. This is why I give people the room to do their jobs. I hire people with the right skill sets and then give them room to succeed." Gus Pagonis, the highly decorated U.S. Army General in charge of logistics during the Gulf War states, "An effective leader needs to have a vision, take care of his people and learn how to motivate them to exceed capabilities without micromanaging."

It sounds simple, but a stage two leader may miss this key point. According to research, it is the immediate supervisor who has the greatest impact on employee job satisfaction.[11] Leaders at this stage need to learn to release the fear of loss.

At stage two, leaders have small Spheres of Attraction because they fear losing something: their jobs, their budgets or their people. They cannot freely engage in meaningful discussions and activities because they have a hidden agenda of holding on to what is theirs. They will not be willing to try new programs unless they see they will gain something. Everything is a "back-scratching" game – "I scratch your back, you scratch mine." If I give you something, what do I get in return? There is no real concern for the betterment of the department; it is about gaining or at least not losing position. At their worst, these leaders can be manipulative, controlling and secretive.

A famous stage two leader was former President Richard Nixon. President Nixon and the Committee to Re-Elect the President (CREEP) were so overcome with fear of losing the reelection they orchestrated a break-in at the Democratic National Headquarters located in the Watergate Hotel. This move ultimately resulted in the president's resignation and prison time for many of his top officials. His fearful thoughts of losing the presidency caused him to make unwise decisions and draw men into his Sphere of Attraction who were willing to break the law and ignore the founding principles of this country.

STAGE THREE: Social

At stage three, leaders have synthesized the lessons from stages one and two. They have moved into the social belonging stage discussed by Abraham Maslow in his hierarchy of needs.[12] Leaders are concerned with being a part of the group. Since they have not completely identified with themselves, they want to belong to the "group think." As such, they will not do anything to be rejected by the group. In meetings they are the people who repeat the same ideas made by others. They will not risk coming up with original thoughts for fear they will be discarded by the group.

Since they have not completely identified with themselves, they want to belong to the "group think."

Another well-known example of a stage three leader is George Wallace. In the TNT movie about his life, some insightful information was revealed. "Throughout his political career, George Wallace would oscillate between the attitudes [of] liberalism, paternal segregation and white supremacist views. In his effort to gain the governorship, Wallace consciously took a hard-line on the issue of segregation and voting rights in order to appease the growing sentiment of racial fear and hatred. In an interview with John Kennedy, Jr., for George magazine (October/November 1995) Wallace conceded, 'Anyone who was running on a platform of integration back then would have been defeated in Alabama. I'm quite sure I would have been defeated if I had supported it.'"[13]

Wallace did not voice his true feelings about racism because he was afraid of being singled out and losing the election. Later in his life, he learned to speak his beliefs and began to mend the harm he had caused to African-Americans – but what if he'd broken with social constraints and spoken up earlier?

At this stage leaders begin to generate notable Spheres of Attraction. People are attracted to them because of the outward success they have attained. Since they have a modicum of success, others seek them for advice on how to achieve in the organization. The challenge is that these leaders can only speak the common opinions of others. Since they have not identified with themselves, they can offer little more than what is written in the company brochures. Leaders at this stage need to release their fear of rejection.

STAGE FOUR: Self-Esteem

Stage four is the point where the desire to lead beyond excellence can be nurtured. Leaders have released the fear of failure, loss and rejection. They are learning to think for and accept themselves. They have been in leadership long enough to realize they have some good ideas. They know if they don't speak up for their ideas, it will come back to them in the mouth of another. So they develop the confidence to speak and act on their own. They are not disturbing to the organization, just the opposite. Because they are developing self-worth, they can begin to appreciate others. For the first time they begin to act from motivations that are not self-protective. Knowing they have value, they are not operating at a fear level. This frees them to be true supporters of the organization and its people.

For the first time they begin to act from motivations that are not self-protective.

Princess Diana was an example of a stage four person. She was loved by the world not because of her position or coercive power, but because of her triumphant journey to herself. When she wed into the royal family, she was burdened not only with satin and lace, but with low self-esteem. Throughout her life she learned to value herself. She did not allow the formality of royalty to separate her from the humanity of sick children or maimed adults. She became known as the "Queen of Hearts" because she showed hers in an otherwise cold and formal monarchy. Princess Diana and other leaders at stage four have larger spheres of attraction because, by revealing their paths to self-worth they, inspire people to value themselves. They have learned how to work within organizations, but not lose themselves; they know how to express their individuality within established environments. In learning to accept themselves, they can genuinely connect with others.

STAGE FIVE: Search

Leaders at stage five have made remarkable advancement on the spiral. They are able to lead at levels beyond the expectations of others. They are not "other-directed," but are "inner-directed." Having learned to value themselves, they are more inclined to trust their own instincts. Although they don't necessarily know why, they intuit something and begin the process to understand. During an interview, Keith Harrison, Global Supply Officer at Procter & Gamble, stated, "Over the years, I have discovered that my intuition is pretty good even if I can't explain why. Guts are smarter than brains. If I have a gut feeling about a situation, I begin to gather information in order to understand what my gut is trying to tell me."

They are more inclined to trust their own instincts.

Stage five leaders are attentive to their co-workers and open to the opinions of others, even if they are opposite of their own. They are viewed as consensus builders because they will search to find common threads on which everyone can agree. They reduce the layers of bureaucracy between themselves and their teams. When asked about Harrison's leadership, one team member explained, "Keith feels no need to dominate others. Before Keith, when anyone was called to the executive suites, it was to be 'called on the carpet' to explain your actions. With Keith, you may get a phone call or an e-mail to see how things are going."

Sheridan Garrison, Member of the Board of the Directors at Federal Express, has classic leadership books lining his shelves. Yet he prefers to lead by his own internal navigational system, what he calls "common sense." With his characteristically southern charm, Sheridan says when it comes to people, every person needs to be recognized and treated fairly.

Additionally, Carlos Santana, world-renowned musician, has exhibited stage five characteristics. He has achieved a great deal of success with his music. With the release of "Black Magic Woman" and other top hits, Santana and his band had fame and fortune. Many band members were content to recreate the same style of music, but Santana was a searcher. He sought ways to blend his musical talents with many other types of music. His desire to lead beyond expectations caused him to leave the confines of his early band. He has now created music that has spanned five decades, outlasted countless musical trends, sold more than 50 million albums, played live to more than 30 million fans, and garnered countless awards and honors[14]. His sphere of attraction is large and reaches across time and generations, as represented by the millions who are still drawn to him and his music. Leaders at stage five are learning to accept their intuitive wisdom.

STAGE SIX: Surrender

Stage six leaders are more inclined to see personal growth and leadership development as the same. They live authentically, making no business decisions they would not make in their personal lives. They surrender to their true desires. Surrender leaders set their own standards. They adhere to Thoreau's famous phrase: "March to the beat of the drum that you hear." In other words, they follow their own leads. What's right for someone else may not be right for them. It is only at this stage that leaders can really bring new perspectives. They are concerned about others and the global environment. They act out of the awareness that humanity is sacred and must be honored whether in their organizations, communities, or across the globe. They manage to reconcile this belief within the guidelines of their lives and businesses.

They live authentically, making no business decisions they would not make in their personal lives.

Take the example of Anita Riddick, founder of The Body Shop. She blends natural ingredients using traditional recipes to create environmentally friendly products. Her company grew from having one store in

Brighton, on the south coast of England in 1976, to selling a product every 0.4 seconds. The company reportedly has more than 77 million customer transactions.[15] The Body Shop is dedicated to creatively balancing the financial and human needs of their stakeholders: employees, customers, franchises, suppliers and shareholders. Additionally, Riddick campaigns for the protection of the environment, human and civil rights, and against animal testing within the cosmetics and toiletries industry.[16] These may seem opposite positions at first glance, but Riddick has found a way of reconciling differences.

"I see no inconsistency in being both a Board Director of The Ruckus Society and an official Ambassador for British Business. Ruckus is a nonviolent, direct-action organization. It uses wit, humor and courage to ensure those who seek to turn a blind eye to the impacts of business operating without a conscience or a heart get the message. That complements my role as an Ambassador for British Business, proving to the corporate world that there is a way of combining profits with principles."[17]

Stage six leaders may have an international Sphere of Attraction. Whether local or global, people are watching and using them as role models to do business differently. Leaders at this stage are accepting total integration of their lives.

STAGE SEVEN: Significant

Stage seven leaders are significant. They act on enlightened self-interest for all. They know themselves to be important to the world and feel they have the responsibility to think and act positively toward all. Their thoughts, dreams and aspirations affect the world.

They act on enlightened self-interest for all.

Nathan Harris, VP of TissueLink, exhibits characteristics of stage seven leaders. He calls his leadership style "Love Leadership." It is so clearly defined that everyone on his team can recite the essence of the philosophy with the statement, "Share the Love." He states, "I am always looking for people I can assist in reaching their true potential. Sometimes these are people the company has all but given up on. And in some cases the person has given up on himself. As a leader, I feel a responsibility to help people."

His leadership philosophy was formed early. As a young manager, working for a Fortune 500 company, he watched senior leadership make poor decisions that cost the company growth and financial stability. The result: good people who had dedicated years to the firm were left unemployed. Walking through empty offices that were once brimming with energetic co-workers, he became acutely aware of the impact leaders had, not only on professional careers, but also on personal lives. He understands his actions can help people and communities.

Leaders reach the seventh stage on the spiral when they are conscious of their relevance to the whole. It is unity consciousness. Here the leaders recognize that their humanity connects them to everyone regardless of culture, race or gender. There is universality to being human. No man is an island. Simply put, it is an understanding of how their actions can affect the world. Leaders at this level intrinsically understand that they impact the work lives of others (employees, customers and suppliers) and indirectly affect those with whom they interact. Creating a productive and positive environment not only promotes a positive work environment, but also contributes to the experiences people take out into the world.

Noted leaders exemplifying stage seven leaders are Sam Walton, the Wright Brothers, Thomas Edison, Bill Gates, Henry Ford, Martin Luther King and Eleanor Roosevelt. These people are humble and don't see themselves any differently than their neighbors. In actuality, they are right. Stage seven leaders are not sitting in the executive suites; they can be seen throughout the organization. They strive to fulfill their dreams in moral and upright manners. While these men and women are not saints, they are dedicated to achieving their goals and helping others reach full potential.

GUIDELINES:
Moving Forward on the Spiral of Influence

HOW TO USE THIS SECTION

This book is written to help you experience a richer and more fulfilling personal and professional life. You have the power to create your perfect life. Previous negative thoughts, feelings of insecurity and identifying with the limitations set by others have prevented you from finding and expressing your true self. You will be guided step-by-step in reconnecting with yourself, thereby creating the life you desire so you can affect positive changes in those you lead.

You have the power to create your perfect life.

Each week you will be presented with a quote selected to move you along the Spiral. The weekly wisdom will help to release your fears and accept your gifts. See Table 2, "Lessons Learned from the Spiral of Influence." Each quote has the capacity to inspire you, make you think and motivate you to act.

Table 2 Lessons Learned from the Spiral of Influence		
STAGE	STYLE	LESSONS LEARNED
1	Survival	Releasing fear of failure
2	Security	Releasing fear of loss
3	Social	Releasing fear of rejection
4	Self-Esteem	Accepting yourself
5	Search	Accepting intuitive wisdom
6	Surrender	Accepting total integration
7	Significance	Accepting self expression

According to Maxwell Maltz in his book *Psycho-Cybernetics,* it takes 21 days to change a habit.[18] For each stage on the Spiral, you will be given 30 days of 10-minute exercises to help you change your thoughts and actions toward your goals. After following the guidelines, you will find yourself releasing old beliefs and reconnecting with your Power and expressing your uniqueness. There are four options for using this section:

1. Begin with the exercises that correspond to the leadership stage determined by the Spiral of Influence Survey.

2. Begin the exercises that correlate with the stage that addresses the lessons you would like to learn. (See Table 2.)

3. Begin with the quotes that inspire you.
4. Start with the first exercise in Stage 1 and continue until you complete the last one in Stage 7.

As a former professor, I have learned the value of repetition for instilling new thoughts. After you have completed the activities for a particular stage, I encourage you to repeat the process. You may also retake the survey to measure how you have progressed. Then do the exercises for your new location on the Spiral. There are four distinct subsections for every stage on the Spiral.

Weekly Wisdoms

In this section you will find a wise quote by a respected leader or philosopher. You are asked to think deeply about the wisdom presented. Drink it in. Think about its relevance to your life, professionally and personally. What does the statement mean to you? How does it affect you? What is your immediate response to the quote? What insights are you able to gain from it? After you have assessed the quote's personal meaning and message to you, read the Insights Section.

Insights

In this section you are given an interpretation of the quote. This is designed to help you reflect on the quote's relevance to key dimensions in your personal and leadership development. After reading the insights section, think about its significance to you. How do you feel about the statement? Do you agree with the interpretation? How does this insight relate to your personal interpretation of the weekly quote? Think about how you can apply the insights from this week's wisdom to your daily life. Read the Action Steps section for more suggestions on implementing these new insights into your life.

Action Steps

Each week you will be given the opportunity to experience the wisdom presented in the quote. The action steps are designed to give you the maximum return for your time investment. Each step takes 10 minutes, but the wisdom you will experience can last a lifetime. Most steps can be performed at your desk. They are designed for you; feel free

Each step takes 10 minutes, but the wisdom you will experience can last a lifetime.

to make some adjustments. If you are asked to sit in silence for 10 minutes, but you feel directed to take a quiet walk, follow your intuition. I encourage you to be diligent in giving yourself the full 10 minutes daily, preferably the same time each day, so that introspection becomes a regular part of your day. After you start to feel the benefits from setting this time aside, you will look forward to it. In the beginning, more dedication is needed. Continue to remind yourself there is no better investment for you or your organization than to be the best leader possible.

People will ask what you did to make such dramatic changes in your life and leadership style.

Personal Observations

At the conclusion of each week you are asked to record what you observed within yourself and the response of others around you. As you continue to follow the weekly program, you will progress up the spiral and develop personally and professionally. You will begin to notice a change in your thinking and actions, which will influence those around you. You will be asked to record your observations in a journal or on the pages in Appendix A. Journaling will enable you to track your changes and the responses of others. This will be an invaluable tool for you and a wonderful way to mentor others. People will ask what you did to make such dramatic changes in your life and leadership style. At that time, you will have this detailed record of your development.

As you turn the following pages, you will be given the map to personal and leadership success. Go ahead and blaze a new path; the signs are clear, and you have all green lights! As you set off, remember the journey will be more adventurous than you can imagine and the destination is *beyond excellence!*

STAGE ONE
Survival

Weekly Wisdom 1.1

"It is the Father's good pleasure to give you the kingdom."

(Luke 12:32)

Insights

"The kingdom represents all your wishes, dreams and goals, whether they are career success, economic security, sound health or loving relationships. It is the true nature of The Father to give you your highest dreams. The Father gives you all you need to achieve success and wealth. Accept that you are not working alone and use this Power to help yourself and others achieve personal and professional goals.

Frankie was a tough kid. He had grown up on the hard side of life. His mother died when he was young and he was shuffled from one family member to another. One day, John, a manager for a leading software company, decided to hire some kids from the neighborhood to show them a way of making money other than stealing and selling drugs.

After one week, Frankie had generated so many complaints, John was asked to speak with him. Frankie walked into John's office wearing blue jeans and a baseball cap, clear violations of the company dress code. John started to tactfully explain that people did not appreciate their personal space being violated, such as going into co-workers' desks. There was money missing from the company coffee fund and...

Frankie interrupted, "Why do all you people think I did these things?" For a few minutes Frankie began to say words that would make a seasoned sailor blush. John calmly but sternly said, "Young man, help me help you." Frankie stopped and didn't utter a word. Then as if his knees gave way, he collapsed into a chair. "No one ever wanted to help me before. I am so used to fighting. I thought I had to fight here too." For the first time Frankie began to realize someone truly wanted to help him.

The Father is constantly working on your behalf to help you create your perfect career and life. This is the basis of the Bible verse, "It pleases The Father to give you the desires of your heart." (Psalm 37:4) You must not stop the source of all good by fighting against it. You fight against the good in your life when you doubt or focus on the negative challenges in life or at work. Rest in knowing there is a higher Power working on your behalf. Your job is to work and act from this knowing. When worry and fear begin to saturate your thinking, shift your thoughts to more positive ones. Think of things that make you happy: your family, future plans, or your favorite hobby. Think about anything that makes you feel happier and more joyful.

Action Steps

Look at your life and be aware of the good that is already present: good friends, healthy family, a lovely home and the modern conveniences of indoor plumbing or microwave cooking. There are many things you may take for granted. Spend 10 minutes daily this week being observant and grateful. Think of your favorite comfortable chair, the hug from a child, the unnamed person who painted the lines on the street for your safety, the person who invented chocolate, or football. For 10 minutes a day, let go of the challenges. Record what is good in your life. For a few minutes smile and be grateful for all the good. Know that it is The Father's desire to give you more.

If you knew you could not fail, what desires would you go after? What do you want to be? What do you want to have? What would you like your team to accomplish? What are your professional goals? What is your financial goal? What are your big dreams, the ones so big you can only discuss them with a select few - or perhaps no one. Remember you can't fail at being you. Accept that it is The Father's good pleasure to give you these desires.

Personal Observations

What did you notice this week that made you grateful? Record your observations. What has The Father already given you for which you are grateful? Did the size of your dreams and goals amaze you? Have your dreams been too small in the past? How different would your life be if you accepted the idea that you could not fail? How would you behave? How would you think? Would you feel freer? Would you be happier? Would you start to relax and stop feeling on edge? Clearly define and record the good you want in your life.

Weekly Wisdom 1.2

"You gain strength, courage and confidence by every experience in which you really stop to look fear in the face. You must do the thing which you think you cannot do."

Eleanor Roosevelt, U.S. diplomat and reformer

(1884-1962)

Insights

Those who are living their dreams looked fear in the face and, with trembling hands and shaky legs, moved through it toward their dreams. You have a yearning to experience more, to have more and to be more.

We all desire to have something we think is out of our reach. For George it was Helen, a beautiful woman who had recently begun working in his department. George so wanted to meet Helen and ask her out for a date, but he never quite had the nerve to do it. Every time he came within a few feet of Helen, all he could do was admire her beauty and grace. After being reminded that confidence was a feeling of hopeFULness, instead of hopeLESSness he began to think of all the possible good that could come by speaking to Helen. He had fun with this, listing more than 30 positive outcomes that could come from meeting Helen. This calmed his fears. He vowed to speak with her the next time he saw her.

On January 10, George was in the break room nursing a cold. He looked up from his lemon tea with honey and saw Helen. Once again, he admired her beauty, but this time he remembered his pact. He tried to reason himself out of the introduction, but he knew now was the time to be confident and trust in goodness. He scooped up his Styrofoam cup and walked over to her. Everything in the room seemed to become silent; all he could hear was his pounding heart – which he was sure everyone in the room heard. But he didn't stop; even when he thought his legs would give way, he moved toward Helen. "Hi, Helen. How are you? I'm George." Noting his stuffy nose she said, "Better than you sound." As George opened his mouth to respond, he felt a tickle in his nose. Before he could think or even clasp his hands to his nose, "Ha cheeew!" There all over his sweater was a long, mucous-colored accessory he had not planned. Helen ran away and he knew that was it. He was an embarrassment and she knew it. As he began to look for tissues, he turned around and, as if in a dream, there stood Helen with a box of tissues and a smile. That began an ongoing joke between George and Helen, which they told at their wedding a year later.

What do you want in your life? Whether it is a promotion, a raise, a loving relationship or new car, you deserve it. Have the confidence to move toward your dreams and goals. Make a pact with yourself to face your fear. You can do it!

Action Steps

This week, write a list of 100 things you would like to achieve if you were not afraid of failing. Ignore the tendency to think within limitations. Just let the ideas pour from you onto the blank page. Remember you can't fail. Reveal your true desires. When you reach 100, group related items under categories such as family, career, health and finances. Date this page and look at it for 10 minutes every day this week. *Feel* yourself having and experiencing your desires – be in your desires. You begin achieving your dreams when you free yourself to list all 100 hundred desires. It is tough to straddle the line between your dream state and reality. It may require a little practice. I assure you it is well worth the investment. At the end of the week, date your list; place it in a calendar along with a written description of how you felt while in your dreams. After six months review the list. You will be amazed at how many of your desires will have come to you through concentrated focus and the powerful attraction of your thoughts.

Personal Observations

This week, become aware of the events taking place related to the items on your list. If new desires occur to you, add them to your list. Remember, you have begun to listen to your true yearnings without the burden of fear. How many yearnings or fears have been with you for more than 10 years? How many items on your list are consistent with childhood desires or fears? It is time to give these desires a true place in your life. Let go of your fears by practicing being in your dreams. If a fear surfaces, let it pass. Return to living in your dream. The fear is powerless to keep you from your dream, unless you focus on it and, through the law of attraction, bring it to you. Release your fears and feel your desires. Be observant and record the observations of the week. When reading your list and descriptions after six months, how much closer are you to realizing your dreams? What can you do to continue moving forward? Record your thoughts.

Weekly Wisdom 1.3

"We all have possibilities we don't know about. We can do things we don't even dream we can do. It's only when necessity faces us that we rise to the occasion and actually do the things that hitherto have seemed impossible."

Dale Carnegie, U.S. writer and speaker

(1888-1955)

Insights

Within you is the ability to conquer your fears and attain your highest goals. Something in you says you can soar above your fears. One of my favorite stories describes a man mountain climbing. He falls off the side of the cliff and, while hanging onto the side, he screams for help. He hears a loud booming voice say, "Yes, my child. I hear you. Just let go and then stand up." After pausing to think for a minute, he screams, "Help! Is anybody else out there?" Later he realized he was only a few feet off the ground. How many times have you thought you were in a difficult situation and in hindsight realized all you had to do was rise to the occasion? The same is true now. It may seem that your career or personal life is overwhelming, but release the fear of failing and stand up. You are only a few feet from achieving the seemingly unachievable.

Action Steps

This week spend 10 minutes each day reminding yourself of the times you stood up. Remember the times you faced a situation instead of assuming failure and running away. When you face a situation it is never as bad in reality as it seems in your nightmares. You can do the impossible. In fact, you have already done the impossible. The odds that you were born are staggering. The fact you were protected and nurtured during your vulnerable early years is utterly amazing. You weren't old enough or mature enough to survive, but you did. Recount the times throughout your life or stories from others that remind you of your ability to surmount the odds. Record these events.

Personal Observations

What did you learn about yourself this week? Record these lessons. How did you feel when you were facing a seemingly unachievable goal? What was the turning point in your success? What did you think about yourself? What did people tell you about your ability to succeed? How did it feel to succeed? What can you bring from that experience to today's situation? Remind yourself: you have succeeded in the past and you will succeed now. Write the affirmation in bold letters and place it where you will see it daily.

Weekly Wisdom 1.4

"Only those who see the invisible can do the impossible."

Alan Cohen, U.S. inspirational author and speaker

Insights

Only those who dare to dream or visualize can achieve the impossible. Scientists tell us that when you visualize, you create invisible thought energy that attract events, people and situations to you. Visioning is a tool for realizing your dreams; many athletes training for competitive events have used it. Venus Williams, one of the greatest female tennis players of all time, was asked by a commentator how it felt to win Wimbledon. She said she had dreamed of it every day and night since she was a kid. The only difference now is that when she woke up she would get to keep the trophy.

A university experiment was designed to test the power of visualization. Students were placed in three groups. Each group member was tested on his/her ability to shoot basketballs. None of the students was a skilled basketball player. Group One, the control group, was told to go home, forget about the experiment and return in 30 days. Group Two was told to practice shooting basketballs for the next 30 days. Group Three was told to imagine or visualize shooting basketballs for the next 30 days.

At the end of 30 days the groups were retested. Group One (told to go home and forget experiment) showed no change in ability. Group Two participants (practiced shooting baskets) improved their scores by 24 percent. Group Three participants (visioning group) improved their abilities by 23 percent (a non-statistical difference between Group 2 and Group 3).[19]

By visualizing your dream, you both see and feel your accomplishment before it materializes. Visualization also identifies where you might focus your actions while your dream is coming into reality.

Action Steps

This week, take 10 minutes each day to visualize your desires. Release your fears. Instead of thinking the WORST CASE scenario, think of the BEST CASE scenario. How does it feel to have your dream? What do you see and feel in your visualization? Where are you? What are you doing? What is the best part of your vision? Who is with you? Have you chosen to purposely exclude anyone from your vision? If so, why?

Make it real. Be in your visualization. If you are leading a highly effective organization and see yourself celebrating a successful year, how does the room look? Is the celebration in the home office or a remote site? Is there food? If so, what kind? Is it formal or informal? Who is at the celebration? Who is missing? Did you receive a raise, a promotion or a new office? What did you do differently to create success for yourself and your organization? Be complete in your imagery. See it and feel it.

Personal Observations

What have you seen this week that reminds you of your visualization? Maybe there was word on a billboard, a line in a movie or even a song on the radio that reminded you of your visualization. Record the events of this week.

STAGE TWO
Security

Weekly Wisdom 2.1

"If you are distressed by anything external, the pain is not due to the thing itself but to your own estimate of it; and this you have the power to revoke at any moment."

Marcus Aurelius Antoninus, Roman Emperor
(121 AD - 180 AD)

Insights

Your mind is the most powerful energy source you possess. Thinking creates feelings, and feelings are like magnets. They attract situations that mirror those feelings. It is not that the events in life are either good or bad; it's how we think about them. If we get what we desire, we term it good; but when we don't, we label it bad. We might label a speeding ticket bad, but if it prevents an accident, it is good. Determine that everything happening in your life is good. It matters not whether you can see the good in it. Every time the sun rises and sets, you have confirmation that everything is happening as it should. As you breathe you are assured you are being supported. Begin to see life as supportive.

Action Steps

This week gain control of your emotions by relabeling events and people in your life as "good." Remember the old adage: "No man is your enemy, no man is your friend; every man is your teacher." Some of life's experiences can be painful and unpleasant, but all have valuable lessons to teach you. From this perspective, what have people or events in your life taught you about yourself? This week relabel all your life events as positive learning experiences. This one step can dramatically change your life.

Personal Observations

How difficult was it to relabel some of your life's events? Were you able to relabel all of them? Which ones do you now see as "good"? Why? Which are you still having trouble calling "good"? Why? Is there anything you can do to see more good in a particular person or situation? What? Record your thoughts.

Weekly Wisdom 2.2

"Greater is He that is in you, than he that is in the world."

(1 John 4:4)

Insights

In this passage John is writing a letter to Christians warning of false prophets who have gone out to deny the Divinity of Jesus Christ. John offers hope by reminding Christians that the Power within them is greater than any false prophets in the world. The message is relevant to all people and religions because false prophets still exist today. They are those who have not yet connected to the Power within themselves.

They are unable to accept the possibility that "all things are possible." (Matthew 19:26 NIV) They live in a world full of limitations. Just as in the days of John, we can recognize them by the words they speak. They tell you why your dream is wrong, unrealistic, impossible or too difficult to achieve. As you read this book and begin to notice positive changes in your personal and professional life, you may encounter those who will tell you why you can't live your ideal life. They will tell you that financial prosperity is contrary to living an honorable and fulfilled life. They will list the economy, job market or shortage of good mates as the reasons your dreams won't come true. At those times I remind you, as John did to the early church, there is greater Power within you.

Within you is a wonderful Power of pure potential – potential to accomplish anything you desire. You can achieve amazing success that is beneficial to you and humanity. The seed of potential needs only nourishment through daily prayer, meditation, positive thoughts and confident actions.

Action Step

Each day this week, sit in silence for 10 minutes thinking on how wonderful you are. Concentrate on your abilities and strengths. What have people told you that you do well? What compliments have you taken for granted? What can you do that comes easily to you which others find difficult? If critical thoughts flash through your mind, simply relax, breathe and let them pass. Then refocus and remind yourself why so many people like and respect you. This week aim to list 20 positive traits about yourself. Review your list daily.

Personal Observations

What positive attributes did you realize you possess? When people complimented you this week, did you feel deserving or uncomfortable? Did you respond with a thank you or some comment suggesting you didn't deserve it? Did you find it easier to compliment others when you were aware of your positive attributes? Continue to list one or two new positive traits about yourself daily. Record your thoughts and feelings.

Weekly Wisdom 2.3

"Nothing great was ever achieved without enthusiasm."

Ralph Waldo Emerson, U.S. essayist and poet
(1803-1882)

Insights

"Enthusiasm" comes from the Greek, meaning, "to be inspired by God." It is the fuel to manifest any great desire. When you are enthusiastic about your life, a business or a project, you ignite a passion that will lead you to excellence. So whether it is a smile, a dance or a waving hand, make a vow to be more enthusiastic.

Donna was an enthusiastic woman, always smiling and energized with ideas. She had begun working in the customer service department leading a group of co-workers, many of whom were several years her senior. The first day at work she held a meeting. Joe, a member of Donna's team, attended. However, he was unhappy about what he called "being passed over" for the leadership position Donna now held. During the meeting he exchanged notes, which caused him and others to laugh. Noticing her first meeting was being disrupted, Donna enthusiastically said, "Joe, thank you for bringing some humor to this meeting. I have decided I would like you to head up our "Double E C Team."

"What is that?" Joe said. "Something you eat? I want hot fudge on mine." The team laughed.

"No, not ice cream, EEC Team," Donna repeated. "It is the Enthusiasm and Excitement Creation Team. For every meeting, you and a select group you identify will design programs, activities, and even games to ignite our excitement about our work. This will spark innovative and creative thinking."

Being enthusiastic herself, Donna found a way of spreading her positive energy to her team and rallying support from someone who planned to be a challenge to her success. Her enthusiasm was infectious. Within 13 months the EEC Team had developed six ways to improve their customers' shopping experiences. Donna's team was featured on the local NBC affiliate, promoting workplace innovation. The free promotion increased sales by 75 percent. Joe received a raise, Donna another a promotion and subsequently customers had a better shopping experience. Enthusiasm had a positive outcome for everyone.

Action Steps

Every day this week practice sincere enthusiasm. In the morning when you rise, think of something that excites you. Did your sports team win? Did your child do well on the spelling test? Did you submit the report on time? Did you finish the project? If you can think of nothing to be excited about, then ponder these points: Did you get out of bed without assistance? Do you have people in your life you care about and who care about you? Do you work in a safe environment? Do you live in a comfortable home? Do you have exciting plans for an upcoming holiday? You do have something in your life that is exciting. Focus on it to create genuine enthusiasm.

Think about achieving your goals. If you absolutely knew you would achieve all your goals, how excited would you be? Be enthusiastic! Expect to have a great day!

This week create a colorful collage. Spend 10 minutes a day collecting and clipping exciting things you'd like to do, experiences you'd like to have and places you'd like to visit. Write words or draw pictures that are thrilling for you. Have fun!

Personal Observations

What did you see this week? What recurrent themes do you see on your collage? What do you really enjoy that you haven't done in a long time? When you were excited, how did others respond? Watch people's attitudes shift when you come into a room. How did you feel this week? How did your days seem – shorter or longer? Did your friends, the people at the post office or the grocery clerks seem happier this week? Remember, your daily experiences begin with the attitude and excitement you bring with you.

Weekly Wisdom 2.4

"When the team performs well the benefit accrues to you, not just the team. Most people don't understand this and try to take the credit. This is not the way. Doing what is best for the team and the organization will eventually help build a successful career."

H. Lee Scott, CEO of Wal-Mart

Insights

Whether we are aware of it or not, we are all connected to one another. All of our bodies need oxygen, iron and carbon to survive. Everyone has experienced joy, success, accomplishment, loss and disappointment. As members of a team we must remember our connectedness. We can all benefit from the lessons our body has to teach us. After all, our individual body parts do not fight against one another. The hand does not consider itself more important or more deserving of attention than the elbow. As team members, we are all important. When the team succeeds, each team member and the organization wins, which translates into a highly effective supply chain.

Look for all the connections in your life. You are a connected team member, family member, etc. What richness is added to your life through these connections? What would be missing from your life if you did not have these connections?

Action Steps

This week spend time being connected to your team, organization and supply chain. Think about the slogan, "One for all, and all for one!" How might you exemplify this in your life? Consider the unity required to be successful. Only through harmony can you reach your objectives. Every day this week practice being a supportive team member. Trust your team to succeed. Allow people freedom to reach their goals. Refrain from giving "friendly advice" this week. Instead, encourage and trust people to find their own answers. Observe the greatness in your team. Congratulate and support team members and, in doing so, know you have paved the way for your own success.

Personal Observations

How did it feel to be a supportive team member? Did you think of other ways to be helpful to your team, your organization or your supply chain? Record the new ideas that come to you. Continue to practice new ways of being a productive team member. Record what you experience by consciously being a supportive team member. How did you feel? How did the team respond to you?

STAGE THREE
Social

Weekly Wisdom 3.1

"We've been able to help our associates to a greater degree than most companies because of what you'd have to call enlightened self-interest."

Sam Walton, Wal-Mart founder
(1918-1992)

Insights

Enlightened self-interest is doing what brings you happiness and joy as long as it doesn't infringe on the rights of others. By pursuing enlightened self-interest, Walton was able to create Wal-Mart, which amassed unprecedented wealth in the retail industry. He became enormously wealthy and made millionaires out of many Wal-Mart associates. Your goal is to joyfully pursue your enlightened self-interest.

Do you think it is impossible to create another Wal-Mart? Well, Walton didn't. He said, "Somewhere out there right now there's someone – probably hundreds of thousands of someones – with good enough ideas to go it all the way. [Wal-Mart] will be done again, over and over."

Perhaps you are the one to do it. Whatever you are to achieve, you must follow your interests. Follow your joy or passions. Whether it's creating a piece of art, a successful business or a loving relationship, you have what it takes to do it. Start following your joy in the pursuit of enlightened self-interest.

Action Steps

Each day this week, take 10 minutes to focus on what you really enjoy. Then do it. Do the things that bring you joy. Don't postpone. Being elated or remembering joyful experiences will give you a wave of energy that will enable you to achieve the seemingly impossible.

Tasha was raised on a Virginia farm. As a young child, she loved to take her saltshaker to the tomato vine and feast right there at the source. Now living in Las Vegas, she recalls those enjoyable days of summer by placing a beautiful saltshaker on her desk.

What could you do to recapture joyful feelings? Is there a picture, an album, a flower or another memento that could ignite your passions? Do something to keep you in a state of joy this week.

Personal Observations

How was your joyful week? What did you do? What did you focus on that reminded you of joyful experiences?

How productive were you this week? Being elated fills you with the enthusiasm that will make the rest of your day or week go smoothly. You will accomplish more things than you imagined. Now you know the secret to productivity and achievement. It is joy.

Weekly Wisdom 3.2

"We have thought that outside things controlled us, when all the time we have that within which could have changed everything and given us freedom from bondage."

Ernest Holmes, founder of the Religious Science movement (1887-1960)

Insights

In times of frustration and disappointment, we often look to someone to rescue us from the unpleasantness. As we wait, we are delaying our freedom. We are our own liberators when we choose to see situations differently, converting our negative thoughts to positive ones. The freedom from bondage is within you. Right now, without moving a finger, loosen yourself from bondage by changing your thinking. You are an individual. You have different life experiences and opinions that sometimes differ from those of the group. This is good. It adds depth to the discussions and a more thorough review because of the perspective you bring. Your individuality makes the team more valuable. Remember, it could not be as successful without your presence. You make a difference.

Action Steps

This week become mindful of how often you are looking to something or someone outside of yourself for help or guidance. Admittedly, asking advice from people you admire can provide you with valuable information. But remember, you also have great ideas and valuable insights. Begin to value them.

For 10 minutes a day this week, record your internal thoughts about a situation that has been preoccupying your thoughts. How do you feel about it? Why is this happening now? Who do you feel is responsible? Now review your notes; see if there is a positive or a negative thought stream. What can you do to make the situation more positive?
(HINT: Change your thoughts.)

Personal Observations

What internal guidance did you receive about making the situation better? Was it helpful? When you followed the guidance, what happened? How did you feel having followed this advice? Did following the advice require you to courageously move out of your comfort zone? Continue to listen to this internal guidance.

Weekly Wisdom 3.3

"A human being is only interesting if he's in contact with himself. I learned you have to trust yourself, be what you are, and do what you ought to do the way you should do it. You have got to discover you, what you do, and trust it."

Barbra Streisand, U.S. actress and singer

Insights

Relationships with significant others – spouses, mothers, fathers, sisters and brothers, are important. But the single most important relationship in your life is with yourself. Are you in touch with yourself? Do you really know what you like? What would you do if you were free to do anything? Do you respect yourself? Are you proud of yourself? Are you happy with the way you live your life? Or do you succumb to the wishes and thoughts of others? Who? Why? What would you do differently if you were free to live your life? When you free yourself, then you will be equipped to move into the world in a way that will cause others to respect and honor you.

Action Steps

For 10 minutes every day this week, look in the mirror and ask yourself: What are the best things about me? In what ways do I treat myself lovingly and kindly? In what ways do I make myself a priority? How do I take care of me? Do I spend enough time with myself? Am I happy? How do I express my uniqueness? Or am I afraid to be myself? Am I free to think my own thoughts? If I felt free to think and act without fear of rejection or criticism, what would I do differently? Do I respect my opinions enough to stand up for myself in the company of others? What are my opinions?

Personal Observations

The exercise described above can be difficult, so be gentle with yourself. How did you feel when you looked at yourself? What do you think about the face in the mirror? What did you see? Do you look happy? What did you learn about yourself? Is there anything you want to change? What? When? Record your observations.

Weekly Wisdom 3.4

"Care about other people's approval and you will be their prisoner."

Stephen Mitchell's interpretation of the Tao Te Ching (ancient Chinese book of wisdom)

Insights

When you deny your true feelings or thoughts to gain the approval of others, you not only imprison yourself, but you withhold your unique gift from the world. What if Galileo had succumbed to the opinion that the earth was the center of the universe? What if Henry Ford had acted on the common belief that a horseless carriage was an impossible idea? Hold to your beliefs. You are created with distinct ideas, experiences and personality. To deny who you are is to delay the progress of humanity. Although you can listen and respect the opinions of others, you must feel free to act according to your internal knowledge. Trust yourself.

Action Steps

This week become conscious of how you are acting when in the company of others. Are you holding back your true opinions and thoughts? How does this make you feel? For 10 minutes stop daily and record your feelings. If you really believe your ideas are important, speak up. Be heard. Free yourself from the bondage of other's opinions. No one's opinion is more important than your own.

Personal Observations

How did it feel to speak your opinion? Were you confident? What will you do differently next time? What did you learn this week about freeing yourself from the opinion of others? Are you still concerned with what others think? Is it preventing you from being you? How might you overcome this reliance?

STAGE FOUR
Self-Esteem

Weekly Wisdom 4.1

"If there is no wind, row."

Latin Proverb

Insights

When you are moving in the direction of your dreams, you may not always sense the support around you. It is important that you continue to remind yourself that you deserve to achieve your dreams. You are worthy of having all your goals. The truth is you are entitled to any success you are able to earn by honest effort. If there is no momentum around your mission, then you must create it. After all, you may be called to produce something never before experienced. Imagine the "wind" the Wright brothers had to generate in building "the flying machine." Just think for a moment how different all lives on the planet would be if they had not chosen to follow their dreams. You are a powerful person. You can single-handedly change situations in your life. In fact, you are the only person who can change your life. As you begin to recognize your self-worth you will generate desirable changes in your personal and professional life.

Action Steps

When you don't have people or situations readily available to motivate you, you will have to be self-motivating. Through the help of inspirational music, poetry, art and sacred writings you can become inspired. You can create a wind that will help you row, for row you must. Your dream is too important to you, co-workers and humanity. You have a unique idea to share. Share it. Step toward realizing it, even if others don't understand. This week spend at least 10 minutes daily listening to inspiring music and writing about three things that make you feel good. Look at old photos that capture great memories, the awards in your office representing past successes, or just simply sit back and laugh at good times with family, friends or co-workers. You are worthy of happiness. More is coming your way, so get used to this feeling.

Personal Observations

How did you feel after listening to inspirational music? Music is a series of vibrations that can literally change your attitude. Poetry, sacred writings and art have the same ability. Draw your feelings in multiple colors after listening to music and reminiscing. Observe what else has the power to positively change your disposition and then incorporate those into your daily life. Record the changes.

Weekly Wisdom 4.2

"They can because they think they can."

Virgil, Roman epic poet

(70 BC - 19 BC)

Insights

The only difference between you and those who are living their dreams is that they think they can. What would you do if you knew you could not fail? Believe you will succeed. Know that you deserve it. Join the higher force within you that is encouraging you to do it. Have the winning attitude.

Lucille Ball, considered one of the greatest comedic geniuses of modern times, is loved and admired by millions. Many are unaware, however, that acting teachers believed her inept. For a while she attended school with Bette Davis. While Bette's work was praised, Lucy's went unrecognized and she was asked go home. Never dismayed and ever confident in her ability she forged ahead, until CBS asked her to star in a new TV series, which later became known as the *I Love Lucy Show.* Lucy believed in herself. She has been noted to have said, "I am not funny. I am brave." You must be self-confident and brave in reaching your goals. Like other successful people you have what it takes to live your dreams.

Action Steps

This week for 10 minutes ask yourself what fears you are avoiding. Look at them. Then complete the statements:

If I were not afraid, I would...

If I did just one small thing that demonstrated my fearlessness it would be…

Afterward I would feel…

Know that like Lucille Ball, everyone has fears; she was just not paralyzed by them. Your strength and success comes in facing your fears. You are powerful; you can make small changes to overcome fears. You deserve to have your dreams. Don't let fear hinder you. This week do one small thing that is fearless.

Personal Observations

What are your fears? What did you do this week to face them? How did it feel to stop running from them? Acknowledging fears is the first step to overcoming them and releasing their hold on your life. Continue to look at what frightens you, but remember to never let it stop you. Record your fears and the actions you took this week to overcome them.

Weekly Wisdom 4.3

"Outstanding leaders go out of the way to boost the self-esteem of their personnel. If people believe in themselves, it's amazing what they can accomplish."

Sam Walton, Wal-Mart founder

(1918-1992)

Insights

The first thing to do in supporting others is to boost your self-esteem. As a leader, if you have any doubts that you are worthy of happiness, success or the best life has to offer, it will be difficult to convince your co-workers of their worth. Freeing yourself of limiting thoughts is your most meaningful work. Negative thoughts about yourself and others must be changed. The most dangerous judgments are the ones you hold about yourself. They lock you in a self-imposed prison, preventing you from reaching your potential and blinding you to the potential of others. Leaders cannot inspire the best in others if their primary need, based on insecurities, is to blame or prove themselves right and others wrong. The result can be low morale, reduced creativity and high job turnover rates. As a leader, you are not only the cornerstone to your personal fulfillment but to the organization's success.

Action Steps

Every day this week spend 10 minutes writing 5 to 10 endings for each statement:

1. If I valued myself just a little bit more, today I would...

2. I can feel better about myself if I would stop...

3. My team/co-workers would feel more valued if I just...

Begin to implement the ideas that come to you.

Personal Observations

What did you write that surprised you? Did you implement the suggestions you received? How was your self-esteem affected? Do you plan to continue incorporating these changes in your life on a more permanent basis? How did it feel to gain insights into ways you can make your team feel more valuable? Were they difficult to implement? What response did you receive from them? Will you continue to implement these changes long-term? Record your thoughts and observations from this week.

Weekly Wisdom 4.4

"The force is within you. Force yourself."

Harrison Ford, U.S. actor

Insights

Within you is the most Powerful force in the universe. Jesus said, "The kingdom of God is within you. Is it not written in your Law, 'I have said you are gods'?" (John 10:34) Housed within you is the most Powerful source known to man. There is a complex chemistry controlling when and in what amounts to dispense magnesium, iron and oxygen. With amazing accuracy and consistency, the perfect combination of nutrients is delivered to the bloodstream. Whether at rest or in the heat of exercise, your body performs innumerable functions that would confound the most sophisticated computer. This same Power is available within your mind to help with every aspect of your life.

Action Steps

Take time every day this week to read John 10:34, then sit in silence for 10 minutes. Listen to what is revealed to you. Record your thoughts.

Personal Observations

What is revealed to you? What are your thoughts and feelings about this revelation? Does this make you feel empowered? Has this revelation changed your viewpoint about who you are? How has your thinking changed this week? What thoughts surfaced as you read the words of Jesus, "you are gods"? Did your mind immediately accept or reject the idea? What does this imply about the current conditions in your life? Are you responsible or is someone else to blame? What can you do differently this week to change your life? To change your leadership? Start small, but begin today making changes. Record your thoughts and feelings.

STAGE FIVE
Search

Weekly Wisdom 5.1

"Restlessness and discontent are the first necessities of progress."

Thomas Edison, U.S. inventor

(1847-1931)

Insights

When we are restless and discontent our creativity starts to flow toward finding a better way, a more productive process and an improved product. Begin to search for better ways. Look at competitors and others. Read more on how to improve the current situation. It's all right to look for unconventional solutions. Also, look at various aspects of your life. In what areas of your life are you discontent? Now begin to consider how you might improve these experiences. Think of how you might change your response to others' actions. If there are things you have direct control over, begin to make changes today.

Action Steps

Find a comfortable place where you can be alone. If you are inside, play soft music, preferably classical; it has been shown to have a positive impact on our moods. Whatever feels good to you is the perfect music. If possible, go outside in nature and listen to its music. Sit on the grass or watch flowing water. Then after a few moments of quiet reflection, ask yourself: How would my perfect life look to me? How would I feel now if all my desires were manifested? How would I assist others if I were a perfect leader? Let your thoughts flow. When your day resumes take the beauty of nature and the joy of your perfect life with you. Now begin to find ways to bring the information from your inner self to your outer world.

Personal Observations

When your day resumed, how did you feel? What will you choose to do differently to become your image of an ideal leader? What thoughts and assumptions will you have to give up? What new thoughts and beliefs will you now hold? How will you change your interactions with others? How will you start to see the perfection in the people with whom you interact?

Weekly Wisdom 5.2

"When I'm trusting and being myself...everything in my life reflects this by falling into place easily, often miraculously."

Shakti Gawain, U.S. inspirational author

Insights

Self-trust is the ability to rely on the wisdom that comes to you from a higher source. It is the desire that doesn't go away. It is your constant companion telling you there is more for you – more joy, more success, more prosperity and more fulfillment. Trust that voice. When you do, you will respect the opinions of others, but you will know that only your opinion matters. You will know you have "insider information" that gives you an edge in all you do. Your intuition is a personal barometer to a more successful life. Respect your guidance; when something feels good and inspires you, move toward it. Conversely, when something feels "bad" to you, move away from it. If it is not possible to avoid it, then change your thinking about it. You have complete control over your thoughts. Absolutely complete control. Be aware of the thoughts you are thinking. Consciously let your positive thoughts guide you. You know something others cannot possibly know because it was revealed within you.

Action Steps

This week trust yourself. Just as with any new practice, start small. Begin by exercising your intuition in small matters; for instance, when you're in doubt about directions to a new location, gently ask yourself which way to turn. When making a choice about a new item on the lunch menu, ask for internal guidance. As you become more in tune with your internal guidance system, use it in other more significant decisions, such as hiring people, resolving conflicts and implementing new programs. You will be amazed at its accuracy. Soon you will find yourself trusting this internal Power on even more important issues.

Personal Observations

What did you notice this week when you started to trust yourself? Don't be concerned if all your decisions didn't turn out as you expected. The ability to trust the Power within you requires practice. For years you have probably given away your Power to others. It takes diligence and practice, but you will develop the ability to listen and trust yourself. When you do – wow! Amazing things will happen to and for you.

Weekly Wisdom 5.3

"An invasion of armies can be resisted, but not an idea whose time has come."

Victor Hugo, French dramatist, novelist and poet (1802-1885)

Insights

Nothing is more powerful than thought. Your thoughts are yours and yours alone. The power of thought will take you to places never before experienced. When ideas come to you, hold onto them. Remember you have the ability to bring them into manifestation. When you think positively, watch those around you suddenly see things more optimistically.

Action Steps

This week, take 10 minutes every day to sit and begin thinking about your personal mission in life. Organizations have mission statements written to keep them focused on achieving their goals. A personal mission statement will do the same for you. To write your statement you must first search within yourself to determine your true desires and ways to express them. It should be short, easy for you to remember, positive and include your life's priorities. It will help you determine which requests to accept and which to reject. If requests are consistent with your mission, accept them; otherwise, decline.

Personal Observations

Record your mission statement. How do you feel about the information you received? Does your mission statement seem complete? Feel free to modify it as you receive more insights and continue to tap into your true desires. These ideas were given to support you. Record all the information you received. Proceed as directed.

Weekly Wisdom 5.4

"The world stands aside to let anyone pass who knows where he or she is going."

David Starr Jordan, U.S. biologist, educator and ichthyologist (1851-1931)

Insights

Self-confidence comes from searching internally for information and trusting what is given. Self-confidence empowers you to achieve your goals. There is an aura of assurance that people recognize, causing them to step aside, allowing you to achieve your goals. According to Cicero, "Confidence is that feeling by which the mind embarks in great and honorable courses with a sure hope and trust in itself."[20] When you have this kind of confidence, nothing in the world will stop you from achieving your goals.

Actions Steps

This week spend 10 minutes thinking about the people who have confidence in themselves and their ideas. They trust their internal wisdom. Remember times you were confident. Compare this feeling to other times when you were insecure. How did people respond to you when you were confident? When you were insecure? Begin to read or watch the biographies of successful people. You will see that confidence is a requirement for success. You will notice that once people become certain of themselves and their ideas, they cannot be stopped. If you were more self-confident, what would you do differently this week? Implement one or two ideas this week.

Personal Observations

What did you learn about the role of self-confidence? Record your observations. How can you have more self-confidence? Begin those activities now.

STAGE SIX
Surrender

Weekly Wisdom 6.1

"If one advances confidently in the direction of his dreams, and endeavors to live the life, which he has imagined, he will meet with a success unexpected in common hours."

Henry David Thoreau, U.S. author, poet and philosopher (1818-1862)

Insights

Stop fighting your true desires; stop fearing you will fail and stop worrying about what others will think. Surrender to your desires. Move confidently in the direction of your dreams. When you free yourself of doubt, you will feel lighter, as if the weight of the world has been lifted from your shoulders. People, situations and information will come to you that will assist you in attaining your goals. You will achieve success sooner than you imagined.

Action Steps

This week surrender to your desires. Don't think OF your dream; think FROM your dream. For ten minutes each day this week, close your eyes and see yourself having your dream. How do you feel? What are you doing? Who is sharing your dream? Where do you live? Do you travel? If so, where do you travel? How are you serving others? Carry the feeling of your dream in your mind throughout the day.

Personal Observations

Each day this week, become actively aware of the signs pointing to your dream. Now that you have started to see life FROM the perspective of having your dream, you may begin to notice people, events and situations that can support you. Record your observations.

Weekly Wisdom 6.2

"The greatest mistake you can make in life is to be continually fearing you will make one."

Elbert Hubbard, U.S. author
(1856 - 1915)

Insights

Your drive to achieve your dream has to be stronger than the fear of making a mistake. Most of us fear making mistakes. But the greatest mistake is to let fear keep you from trying. Surrender to your goal. Let positive thoughts of achievement replace those of fear and failure. If you never move toward your goal, you will certainly never achieve it. Perhaps life will throw you events alerting you to make adjustments. But even these put you one step closer toward achieving your dream.

In her professional life, Sally Jesse Raphael was fired more than a dozen times as host of various talk shows, but she did not allow fear of failing prevent her from trying. With each failure came a lesson she transformed into personal wisdom. Eventually, Raphael became host of the longest-running daytime talk show in history, The Sally Jesse Raphael Show.

Action Steps

For the next week, take 10 minutes a day to think of the things you have always wanted to do. What have you wanted to experience for yourself? If you were able to fully integrate yourself into your work, what would your career look like? What kind of work would you do? Start to think of what you would do if you were living your ideal life. Where would you begin? Then move courageously in that direction. As you surrender to your true desires, think of others who have made similar choices. They can become your personal coaches. Search online, visit the library or watch documentaries for them. Their lives will encourage you if mistakes occur, which are simple adjustments to your plan. When you need guidance, ask yourself if "John Smith" were here, how would he handle this situation? You will be amazed at the information you receive. If the guidance feels good, follow it. If not, ask again or ask another coach.

Personal Observations

What have you seen this week that makes you more driven to achieve your professional goals and personal dreams? What new guidance did you receive this week? How did you feel about the information? Did you follow it? Record your observations.

Weekly Wisdom 6.3

"If you want to succeed you should strike out on new paths rather than travel the worn paths of accepted success."

John D. Rockefeller, U.S. industrialist and philanthropist (1839-1937)

Insights

The only way to make a difference in your life and in the world is to surrender to your own intuition. Within you is an internal compass to successfully guide you through all life's events. Following this invisible guide requires courage. You may not always see the complete picture, but you will receive the incremental steps. If you have the courage and the persistence to follow this internal guidance, you will set out on a path that leads to your personal best and inspires other as well.

Action Steps

You have a unique position to fill. There never has been and never will be another person with your specific gifts. If you don't have the courage to follow your dream, which inherently is a gift to the world, there will be a void for all of humanity. Sit in silence for 10 minutes each day and ask to receive insights on what you can do to improve your life and career. Record the insights you receive. Then be courageous; list one or two and implement them this week.

Personal Observations

How did you feel when you heard the guidance of your intuition? Were you given new information or was it something you've known for a while? As you recorded the information, did you receive any additional understanding? How did it feel to actually list one or two items to complete this week? Did it seem possible or difficult to complete? What was the actual experience implementing the information given? What feelings or additional information did you receive as you implemented the guidance? How was your life or career impacted? Record your thoughts and feelings.

Weekly Wisdom 6.4

"A man's true estate or power and riches is to be in himself, not in his dwelling or position or external relations, but in his own essential character."

Henry Ward Beecher, U.S. abolitionist and clergyman (1813-1887)

Insights

Your greatest asset is your connection to your powerful intuition, not your position, income or relationships with others. When you understand this and surrender to this inner wisdom, your income, your positions and your relationships will flourish. They will be based upon healthy self-reliance and expression, not on insecurity and need. As you know yourself and express your individuality, you will make a significant impact on your world and those around you.

Action Steps

For 10 minutes every day this week, think about the uniqueness you bring to the world. Think of ways you can better express your uniqueness to others. It's important that you fully express your opinions, ideas and talents. Think of the impact Elvis Presley, the Beatles and Sean "P. Diddy" Combs have had on the world just by expressing their distinctiveness. How bland would music be without these individuals trusting and expressing their distinctive interpretations? Think this week how you can bring more of your own individual ideas and thoughts to your environment. Begin small, but strive to integrate more of yourself at work and in your personal life this week.

Personal Observations

How did you feel being more integrated? Can you think of other ways you can blur the boundaries between your personal and professional life? Continue to blend both aspects of your life. How does it feel to be more authentic? Record your thoughts.

STAGE SEVEN
Significance

Weekly Wisdom 7.1

"We must be the change we wish to see in the world."

Mahatma Gandhi, Indian ascetic and nationalist leader (1869-1948)

Insights

If we want our lives to be filled with more peace, joy, kindness and compassion then we must begin within ourselves. Start this week to practice being more loving and kind to others and yourself. You will be amazed at the peace and joy you will find increasing in your life. You can then spread these experiences around as you move in the world.

Action Steps

Every day this week practice kindness by being kind to all you meet. Each day meditate by sitting in silence and bringing your attention to your heart. Listen; feel your pulse and gently breathe in. Hold your breath for four seconds, then breathe out slowly. Repeat four times. Soon you will experience calmness. Carry this feeling with you every day; enter the world and practice kindness in all your personal and professional interactions. The day-to-day events in your life will become filled with more love and harmony. When you find yourself feeling anxious, angry or frustrated, return to focusing on your heart and breathe. Breathe deeply and slowly until you feel calm again.

Personal Observations

How many acts of kindness did you demonstrate this week? How many acts of kindness did you receive this week? Record any internal revelations you received through the practice of loving kindness. Practice replacing the stress in your life with calmness.

Weekly Wisdom 7.2

"As you become more clear about who you really are, you'll be better able to decide what is best for you—the first time around."

Oprah Winfrey, U.S. actress and talk show host

Insights

All great thinkers and achievers in the world have at one time been considered unconventional. This is because they've had an inner connection that spoke to them in a manner incomprehensible to others. There is a saying: "Those dancing were thought to be insane by those who could not hear the music." You are dancing to your music. It may communicate things to you that others cannot understand, but it is fine. The message is for you to use in benefiting yourself and others. In time, as with all great men and women, the rest of the population will understand what you already know. So don't worry if you are misunderstood. Just move forward confidently, understanding you are simply ahead of your time.

Action Steps

This week, think about great visionaries: Henry Ford, Thomas Edison, Alexander Graham Bell, Bill Gates and others who had to overcome skepticism. They were misunderstood because they were attempting something never witnessed before. People had no frame of reference for what they were advocating. But these visionaries continued to create according to their dreams, thereby improving the lives of everyone.

As you think of visionaries or others whom you admire, list three to four positive traits for each individual. Then go back and circle traits repeated across the individuals listed. Consider their similarities and recognize that you have these same positive attributes. Yours may be dormant, but you have them. If you didn't have them you couldn't recognize them in others. For example, when Christopher Columbus' ships approached the Caribbean Islands the inhabitants couldn't see them, although the armada was in plain view. They couldn't recognize it because they had no frame of reference for ships. Only after their wise men explained what was coming, could they see it. If you didn't have the same traits you could not identify them. This week practice expressing more of your positive traits you've noticed in others you admire.

Personal Observations

Which visionary did you think about this week? Why did you select him or her? What do you admire about them? How did you feel when you realized you have the same attributes? Have you accepted this? Why or why not? How did you express these qualities this week? How did it feel? How did people respond to you? How do you plan to implement these qualities daily?

Weekly Wisdom 7.3

"The wise and moral man shines like a fire on a hilltop, making money like a bee, who does not hurt the flower."

Pali Canon (sacred literature of Buddhism)

Insights

The wise and insightful person is prosperous. "Making money like a bee" implies being profitable, productive and helpful to all. The bee, feeding on the nectar, becomes full, provides honey to feed others in the hive and helps the flower to bloom into its full beauty. Leaders "making money like a bee, who do not hurt the flower" help people develop their full potential. These leaders have an aura around them that shines brightly and attracts success. Think of those who were driven to achieve and helped mankind, like Paul Newman, Florence Nightingale, Jonas Salk and Oprah Winfrey.

Action Steps

Consciously be aware of how you are interacting with others. Be a little more kind to people. When interacting with others think on their positive attributes. Give everyone you meet a gift of a truthful compliment, a gentle pat on the back or some other encouraging sign. This week consciously learn the names of five people you see regularly. Then acknowledge or thank them by name.

Personal Observations

Watch how people respond to your positive thoughts about them. Do they become more thoughtful or accommodating? Do they also give you the gift of a truthful compliment, a kind word or a pat on the back? How did you feel this week about those you met? Were they more helpful and encouraging? How did people respond when you called them by name? How did you feel remembering their names? Record your observations.

Weekly Wisdom 7.4

"A business absolutely devoted to service will have only one worry about profits. They will be embarrassingly large."

Henry Ford, U.S. automobile industrialist
(1863-1947)

Insights

Customer service begins with your co-workers. As the leader your role is to create an environment where everyone feels free to be themselves and empowered to succeed. Every day, communicate your appreciation for all they do. Expect great things from them, then watch them treat customers well. You and your co-workers will experience the Pygmalion Effect, or a self-fulfilling prophecy. You will have high expectations for them and they will perform exceptionally. This effect has been researched many times. The results consistently show the effect our thoughts and expectations have on the success of others and an environment's productivity.

Action Steps

Each day this week, make a conscious effort to support the partners with whom you work. Congratulate them. Encourage them. Expect great accomplishments from them. Commend yourself on being a positive and productive force within the organization and supply chain. How did it feel to concentrate on good behavior? How did co-workers respond? Record the good things you observed or heard about your co-workers. Share this with them.

Personal Observations

How did you feel this week? How did your co-workers and supply chain partners respond to your encouragement? How did you feel about yourself when you expected the best from them? Was the environment happier? More productive? What impact did your positive expectations have on co-workers? Supply chain partners? Customers? Record your observations.

ENDNOTES

1 www.ideafinder.com/history/inventors/kamen.htm

2 For complete interviews with leaders researched for this study visit www.williamsresearch.com.

3 A&E Video Biography (1997), *Sam Walton: Bargain Billionaire.*

4 Sam Walton, *Made in America: My Story* (1992) Doubleday, New York, NY.

5 Quotes from *Parade Magazine*, September 8, 1996, P.4-5.

6 Boulay, *Art Leadership Focus, Malden Mills: A Study in Leadership*, 1996 Quality Mentor Newsletter.

7 Bennis, Warren, *On Becoming a Leader*, Addison-Wesley Publishing Company, NY, NY (1995).

8 Wheatley, Margaret J. and Myron Kellner-Rogers, *a simpler way*, San Francisco: Barrett-Kohler (1996).

9 Lindahl, Lawrence, "What Makes a Good Job," *Personal*, Vol. 25, January 1949.

10 *Webster's Revised Unabridged Dictionary*, ©1996, 1998 MICRA, Inc.

11 Lindahl, Lawrence, "What Makes a Good Job," *Personal*, Vol. 25, January 1949.

12 Abraham Maslow, *Maslow on Management*, John Wiley & Sons (1998).

13 TNT information from the Movie *George Wallace.*

14 www.carlossantana.com

15 The Body Shop Website, www.the-body-shop.com, May 26, 2003.

16 Ibid

17 Ibid

18 Maxwell Maltz, *Psycho-Cybernetics*, Pocket Books, New York, NY (1974).

19 Stretton Smith, Stretton Smith, 4T Prosperity Program, The 4T Publishing Co., Carmel, CA.

20 Ted Goodmans (editor), *The Forbes Book of Business Quotations: 14,173 Thoughts on the Business of Life*, 1997.

RECORD YOUR THOUGHTS

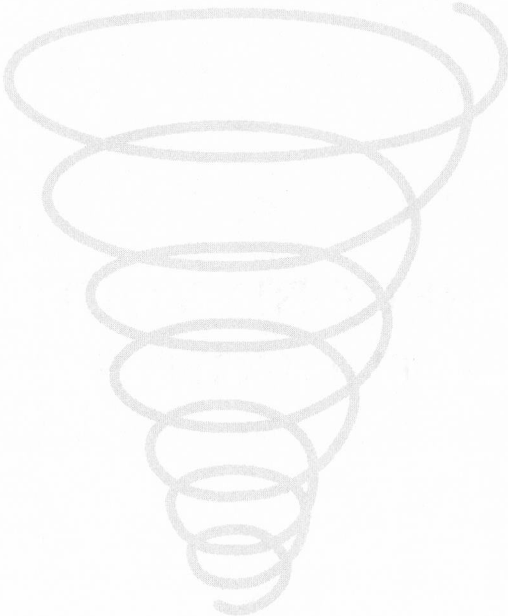

Record Your Thoughts

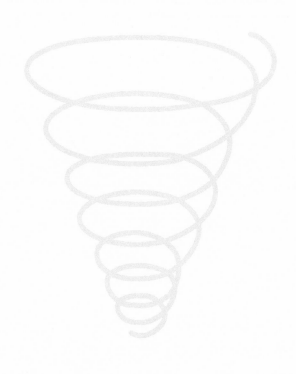

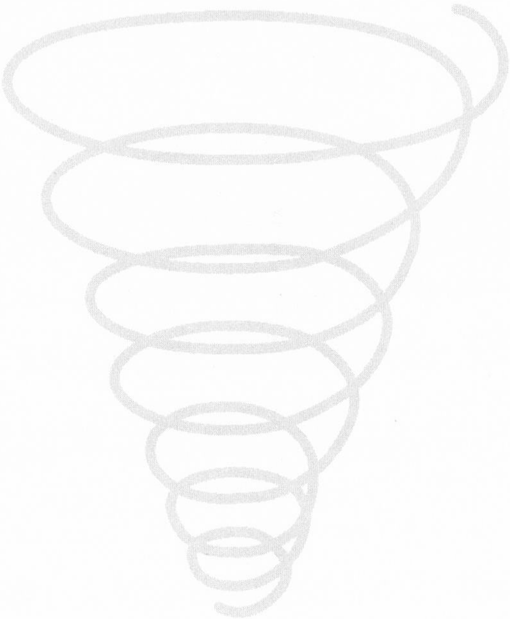

Record Your Thoughts

Record Your Thoughts

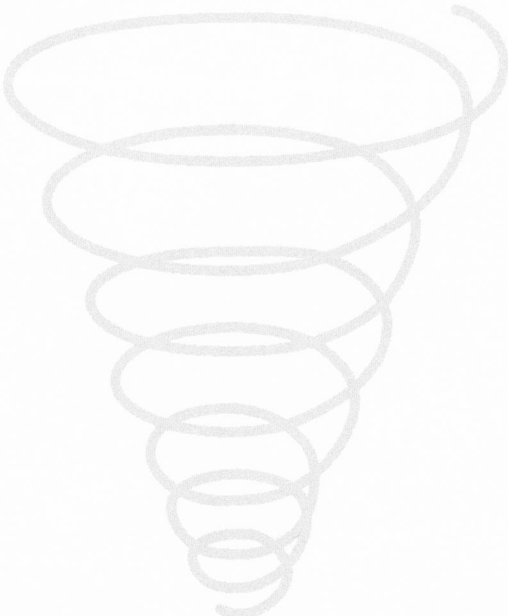

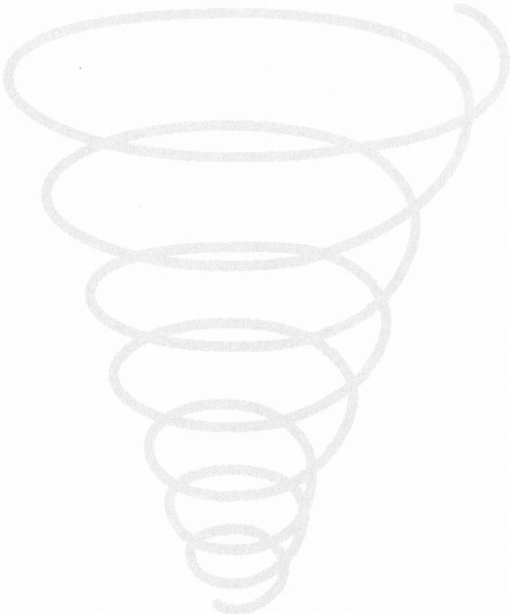

Record Your Thoughts

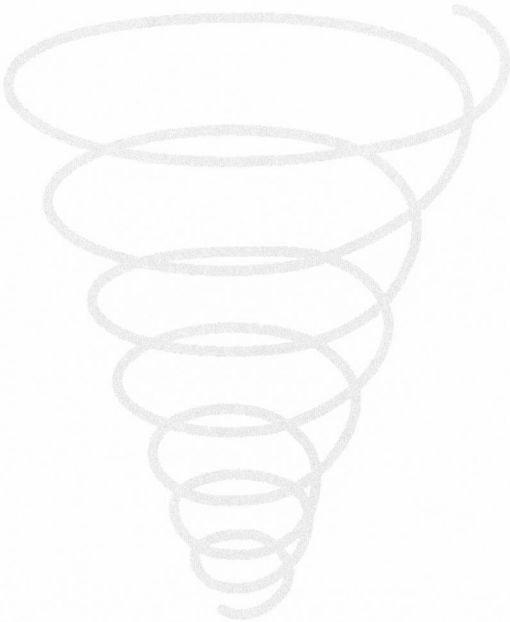

Record Your Thoughts

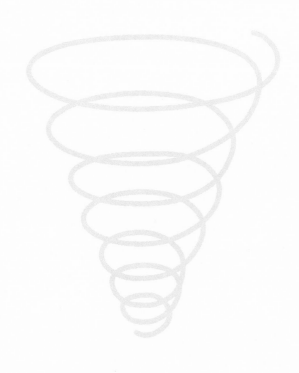

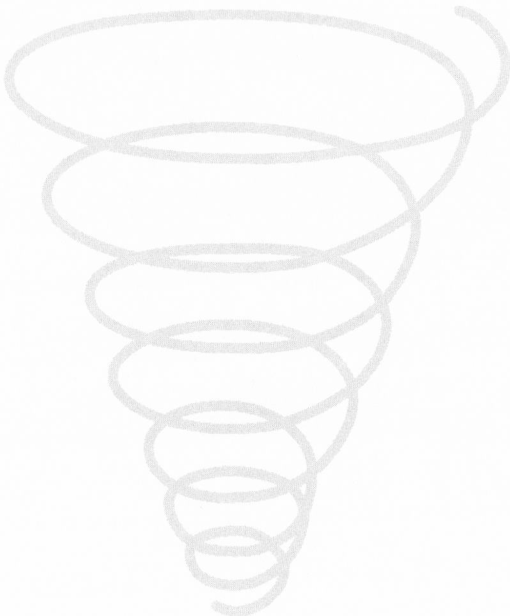

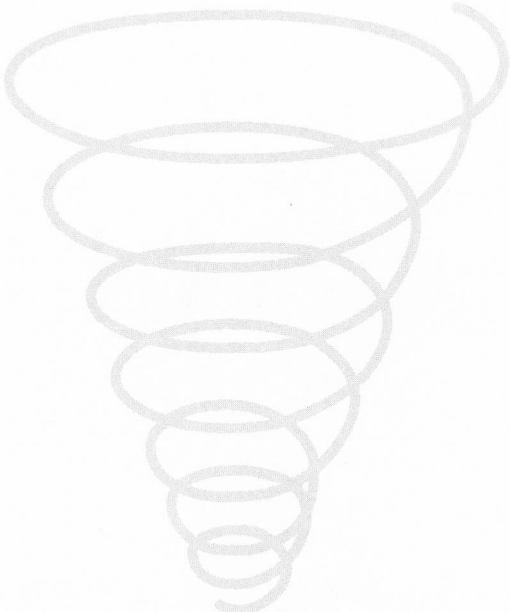

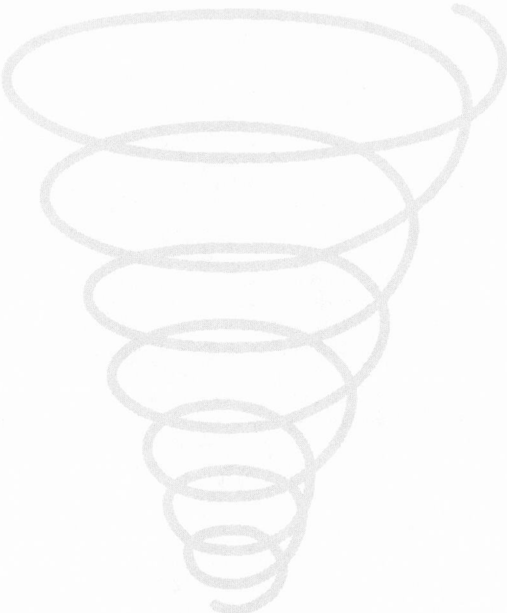

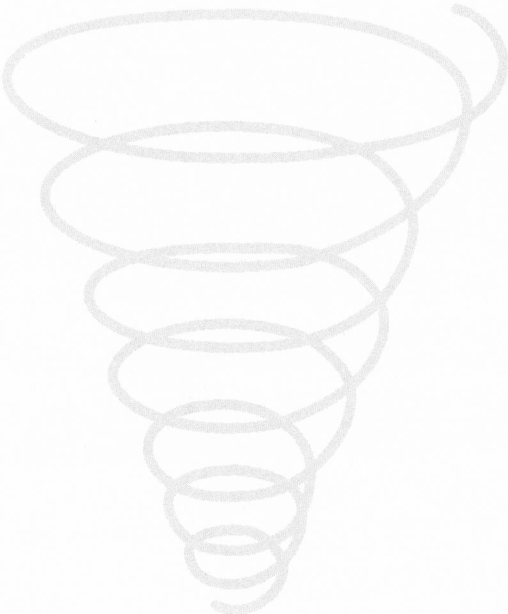

Record Your Thoughts

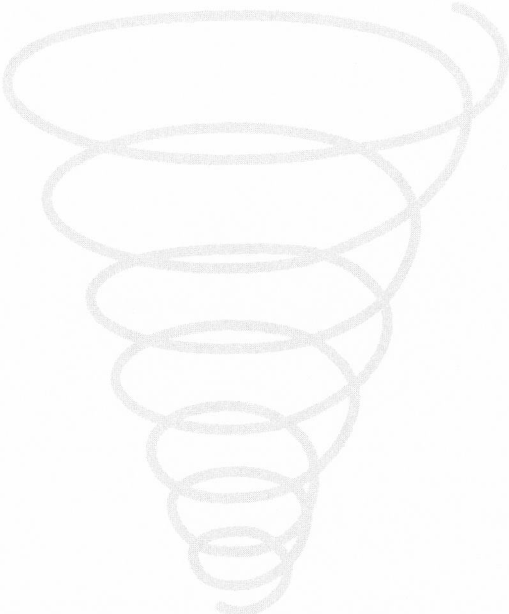

Foreword to Discussion Questions:

An important element in achieving your goal is having a supportive group. Toward that end, you are invited to select three or four people you feel encourage you in attaining your goals. Ideally, these people are committed to leading beyond excellence and you can support them in achieving their goals. Together you will form a Leading beyond Excellence And Development (L.E.A.D.) Team. Weekly L.E.A.D. Team meetings are recommended to provide an excellent boost to your daily exercises. The meeting length can vary from a lunch hour to an evening session based upon team member time constraints. You are, however, encouraged to set a specific date and time for your weekly meetings to ensure other events do not take precedence. Make L.E.A.D. Team meetings and daily exercises a priority and you will be amazed by how quickly you achieve your goals.

On the following pages you will find questions to spark the weekly discussions.

Discussion Questions:

Achieving Goals

Three major goals I am aiming to achieve in life are:

1.______________________________________

2.______________________________________

3.______________________________________

Write a positive statement in the present tense for each of these goals. Example: "I am successful now." If that seems too bold, try: "I am willing to be successful now."

1.____

2.____

3.____

Recite the statements from the previous page 20 times daily. During each weekly L.E.A.D. Team meeting say them to your team. The team is to respond, "Yes, (your name), (your positive statement)." Example: "Yes, Mary, you are successful now!"

I am worthy of achieving my goals because:

I want to achieve my goals because:

This will benefit my life by:

It will benefit the lives of others by:

When I achieve these goals my life will look like:

Describe your new life using your senses. In other words, what do you see, hear and feel? Share this image with your

L.E.A.D. Team. Write this down and read it 20 times daily.

Past Accomplishments

I know I can achieve these new goals because I have already improved my life by:

____

____

____

____

____

____

____

____

____

The goals I have achieved in the past are:

____

____

____

____

____

____

____

____

My five greatest successes to date are:

1.____

2.____

3.____

4.____

5.____

Admirable People

The people I admire, dead or alive, whom I know or have never met are:

I admire them because:

The traits you admire in others are within you. They may be dormant. The first step in awakening these traits is acknowledging that you possess them. Thus, when looking at the qualities you admire in others, circle those that re-occur. You possess these same qualities. Everyday write a statement or visualize yourself using these traits.

Refusing to Settle for Less

Sometimes I settle for less in my life when I:

I have been standing in the shadow of:

In the past I have chosen to stand in their shadow because:

I now choose to step out of the shadow as I achieve my goals and desires. When I catch myself settling or standing in someone's shadow I will:

____

____

____

____

____

____

____

____

____

Reserve My Energy

Achieving my goals is my priority. I will focus my energies on them. Ways I will stop allowing my energy to be drained are:

____

____

____

____

____

____

____

Acknowledging and Releasing Fears

The fear(s) I will have to address in reaching my goal is/are:

____

____

____

____

____

____

____

____

The circumstance that first led to this fear was:

____

____

____

____

____

____

____

____

____

____

____

____

____

I am now willing to let my goal instead of my fear lead me. The next time I feel this fear I will:

Share with your L.E.A.D. Team. They can encourage you and offer advice. Often people are dealing with the same or similar fears. You are not alone. Be assured you can overcome your fear with help. Prepare to discuss your progress weekly.

Action Steps

Realistically I can achieve my goals by (date):

____

____

Starting from the date listed above, work backward to today. Ask yourself, what three actions will I take this week toward achieving my goals? Update the three goals weekly.

1.____

2.____

3.____

The weekly plan for achieving my goal is:

Share this week with your L.E.A.D. Team. They can help you to be accountable.

Developing Leaders Beyond Excellence

You have stepped solidly on the path to leading beyond excellence.

We are here to further assist you in developing your leadership excellence.